Great Yorkshire
Shopping

SUSAN PRESTON

Dalesman

Dalesman Publishing Company, Stable Courtyard, Broughton Hall, Skipton, North Yorkshire BD23 3AZ
www.dalesman.co.uk

First Edition 2000

Text © Susan Preston 2000

Main cover photography © Bill Wilkinson; central photograph of York Shambles © Deryck Hallam

Illustrations and maps: Bluestone Design Group

A British Library Cataloguing in Publication record is available for this book

ISBN 1 85568 185 4

Printed by Amadeus Press, Cleckheaton

Great Yorkshire Shopping

SUSAN PRESTON

For my family, especially Neil who for once hasn't protested at my shopping expeditions!

Contents

Introduction

To shop is most definitely one of the things I was born to do. I hold my hands up now and confess that I just love it. I am not referring to the dreaded trolley dash round the supermarket, with the children playing up and picking up endless unwanted items when I am not looking, but to civilised, leisurely shopping in choice establishments selling quality goods.

Shopping for me, as I suspect it is for many others, is a pastime. I enjoy exploring shops which are just that bit different – especially when they're found in an attractive setting. High street shopping has its place, but the over-commercialised nature of many town centres doesn't satisfy the need in me for something other than glitz. Thankfully, living in Yorkshire, I don't have to travel far to find what I want. The county is teeming with glorious shops full of character – far removed from the comparative sterility of many high street outlets; shops where you can celebrate quality, craftsmanship and an integrity often lacking today. I suspect there are fewer such places now than in the past which is even more reason to treasure them and the things they sell.

I have delighted at finds made during researching this book and at visiting favourite places such as York and the Dales and discovering many beautiful little villages and hamlets that were previously unknown to me. Places such as Hutton-le-Hole in the North York Moors which are stunning in their natural beauty and offer the visitor a true escape from town and city life. They are also home to unexpected shopping discoveries.

On my travels I have enjoyed chatting with the people responsible for many of the treasures you will find within these pages and thank them now for their time and refreshments. All have businesses to

INTRODUCTION

run, but still find time to talk to visitors. It is a great attraction of the shops I have selected that in most cases you actually deal with the owners and the people who create the products sold.

Yorkshire is a great county and presents endless opportunities to visitors. It has its fair share of lively, action-packed town centres but also excels in its glorious countryside. Either option offers something special – York its magical cobbled streets and stunning architecture; Harrogate a unique classy style and appeal; the coast its seaside charm and the Dales their limestone scenery and unspoilt villages. There are heather-clad moors to roam, and Brontë and 'The Last of the Summer Wine' country to explore.

Wherever you go the distinctive nature of your surroundings can be found reflected in the quality and range of goods and tasty fare on offer. In the main these will not be factory-produced items seen on every high street far and wide, but unique products found only in Yorkshire – items for which the much-banded and over-used 'exclusive' tag can for once be legitimately applied. Often you can witness the product being made, from fabulous traditional rocking horses and bespoke footwear to guitars, rope, wine and exquisite jewellery.

Along the way there are a few Yorkshire 'institutions' to pay homage to – something you will do more than gladly at the likes of Bettys Café Tea Rooms, John Farrah's of Harrogate and Whitaker's of Skipton – over and over again! Other shops share the same long-established and deep-rooted association with Yorkshire and have fascinating histories.

The shops in this book will help give you a rare shopping experience, and on your journeys you will doubtless encounter other finds. For this is by no means a definitive guide. There are many industrious people in the region, lovingly creating items for our delight. While I have discovered a large number of these, there are still many you can take great pleasure in stumbling across yourself.

I hope you enjoy visiting the shops I have chosen for their

INTRODUCTION

distinctive and unique appeal. If you ever need a gift for someone special I suggest you use this book to help you make the perfect choice. I have seen some stunning creations at the shops featured here and know they would make much-appreciated presents – and you can always treat yourself as well, of course!

I have had great fun compiling this book and am sure it will add an exciting and refreshing new dimension to any visit to Yorkshire.

SUSAN PRESTON

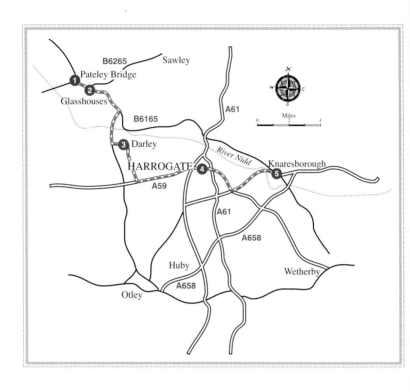

1 Pateley Bridge
Dianne Cross Ceramics
Brian and Joy Loomes
The Oldest Sweet Shop in England
David South

2 Glasshouses
Yorkshire Country Wines

3 Darley
Darley Mill Centre

4 Harrogate
Allens
Bettys/Taylors
John Cornforth
John Farrah's
Ogdens
Woods

5 Knaresborough
Henshaw's Arts and Crafts Centre

Harrogate & Nidderdale

Introduction

This area offers visitors a delectable mixture of stylish shops, cosmopolitan ambience and beautiful countryside that never fails to impress.

I often visit Harrogate. As a town it has everything and for sophisticated shopping in a relaxed, welcoming environment you will find few, if any, better places. There are not only exquisite shops, cafés and restaurants, but also beautiful gardens and architecture which give this elegant spa town a unique quality.

If you have money to spend there are many fabulous individual shops to entice you to part with it in Harrogate, and if you don't you will enjoy browsing almost as much. The town's wealth of clothes and shoe shops is a constant draw, as too are its fine antique outlets.

For many people a visit to Harrogate is not complete without sampling fine food and drink at the famous Bettys Café Tea Room. When the pianist is playing and you are looking out over the magnificent Montpellier Gardens eating some of Bettys scrumptious fare you will thank me for this recommendation.

Other shops that have long associations with the town and fascinating histories, include Ogdens the jewellers and Farrah's – famous for its yummy toffee. Farrah's has also now opened a chocolate factory and is making its own range of delicious chocolates.

Just a few miles from Harrogate is Knaresborough, a quaint market town where you can not only enjoy shopping but can take a boat out on the River Nidd. Here you will find The Oldest Chemist Shop in England that dates back to 1720 and now belongs to John Farrah's of Harrogate.

Not far away, you can find The Oldest Sweet Shop in England at Pateley Bridge which on its steep high street offers visitors local crafts, shops and tearooms aplenty.

❶ *Pateley Bridge*

Dianne Cross Ceramics

Dianne Cross is one of a band of talented craftspeople based at King Street Workshops at Pateley Bridge. She produces a range of brightly decorated wheel-thrown functional stoneware pottery, including wonderful teapots and cups and saucers, and also some equally eye-catching decorative pottery.

Dianne has been making pots since 1981, first in Otley and since 1992 at King Street Workshops. Here in an attractive courtyard setting you can also see the fascinating craft of glassblowing at Sanders and Wallace, some stylish jewellery by Debby Moxon and Ian Simm, and also John Dix terracotta pottery and Oak and Country Furniture.

Opening Times Dianne's workshop is open on Mondays, Wednesdays, Fridays and Saturdays, generally from 10am to 5pm. Workshops generally open 10am to 5pm most days all year.

Address King Street Workshops, Pateley Bridge

Contact 01423 712054

Brian and Joy Loomes

For antique clocks you should look in the direction of Brian and Joy Loomes. From their farmhouse home they run a specialist business with Brian using his enormous expertise to ensure customers get only the very best.

For as well as being a dealer, Brian is today's best-known and most widely published author in the field of antique clocks. Indeed, he has written no less than 21 books on clocks and hundreds of articles in antiques-related publications worldwide. Two recent books are Clockmakers of Northern England and Brass Dial Clocks which includes a detailed survey of every known clockmaker working in the 17th century in each county with the type of work he made. Signed copies are available from Brian or by post, or unsigned copies through booksellers and newsagents.

The business was established in 1966 and deals principally in grandfather clocks, of which it holds probably the largest stock in the country of pre-1830 examples. There are normally about 60 grandfather clocks in stock (doesn't that create a wonderful visual picture and imagined sound?), and all are genuine items in guaranteed working order.

There is also a constant stock of all Brian's books that are currently in print, which you could well be tempted to buy. Several of his works have become standard texts and are used by collectors, dealers and museums throughout the world.

Opening Times Brian and Joy Loomes is open by prior appointment five-and-a-half days a week.

Address Calf Haugh, Pateley Bridge

Contact 01423 711163

The Oldest Sweet Shop in England

Prepare for a trip down memory lane (and perhaps a trip to the dentist!) after a visit to The Oldest Sweet Shop in England at

Pateley Bridge, where if you are like me and have a sweet tooth you will think you have died and gone to sweetie heaven!

Established in 1827, this shop stocks most of England's oldest traditional sweets. Foreigners visiting the shop are often so taken with its contents that they have items posted to them. The shop offers a mail order service.

The sweets found here include all the old greats such as Rhubarb and Custard, Humbugs, Midget

Gems, Aniseed Balls, Kopp Kopp's, White Mice, Liquorice Root and Original Pontefract Cakes. The shop's owner Dianne Rocks told me that Americans went wild for the liquorice. There are also Farrah's of Harrogate toffees and Whitakers of Skipton products on sale.

The shop has managed to survive hard periods. During the Second World War only cough tablets and liquorice root were available.

Also note the shop's timbers and beams – they came from one of King Henry VIII's war ships, and its till dates back to the 1850s. In addition to the sweets a variety of other goods are sold, including local farmhouse produce, Yorkshire Country Wines and specialist beers. A hamper-making service is available.

Opening Times 8am to 5pm seven days a week.

Address 39 High Street, Pateley Bridge

Contact 01423 712371 • www.nidderdale.co.uk

David South

If you like old furniture and have searched everywhere for the perfect wing chair or chaise longue to no avail, this is just the shop for you.

This wonderful find is a family-run business that sells antique and period furniture and offers a full upholstery and restoration service. Just round the corner from the shop is a large showroom packed to the brim with old chairs and sofas that are suitable for restoration and reupholstery and will make stylish additions to any home.

The shop has an extensive range of upholstery fabrics, both contemporary and traditional designs, and offers a bespoke furniture making service. Its workshops create mainly traditional designs, including wing chairs, a winged sofa, and a tub chair.

Opening Times 9am to 5.30pm Monday to Friday, 9am to 5pm Saturday. Closed Sundays.

Address Kings House, 15 High Street, Pateley Bridge

Contact 01423 712022 • www.davidsouth.co.uk

 Glasshouses

Yorkshire Country Wines Gallery and Antiques

Yorkshire Country Wines is a small business producing traditional country wines, started over a decade ago by husband and wife team Richard and Gillian Brown. They are based in the vaulted cellars of a 19th century flax mill in an idyllic location overlooking the River Nidd in Glasshouses – 12 miles from Harrogate. Here they use fresh flowers and where at all possible local fruits and vegetables to ferment in a traditional way a range of country wines with their own distinctive flavours and styles. These include the popular Elderberry and Elderflower.

They produce approximately 25,000 bottles each year, which are sold mainly in Yorkshire, a great many of them to visitors who join a winery tour with tasting.

Some years ago the couple converted another part of the disused cellars into a gallery selling antique oak and country furniture with contemporary pictures and ceramics. The turbine room was also converted into a wine tasting and sales area for visitors. This houses a large and impressive water turbine in the floor.

More recently the Browns opened a tearoom with three distinct areas of seating – the cosy snug with a fire and old settles, the conservatory which previously housed the steam engine, and finally (weather depending) the dappled terrace with large stone tables overlooking the river. This area has been described as 'heaven'.

Opening Times 11.30am to 4.30pm, Wednesday to Sunday. Open weekends only from Christmas to Easter.

Winery Tours Friday and Saturday only at 11.45am. £2.50 per person.

Address Riverside Cellars, The Mill, Glasshouses, Harrogate. Glasshouses Mill is signposted from the crossroads of the B6165 Harrogate to Pateley Bridge Road. Drive down through the village, passing the mill entrance, until you reach the Riverside car park.

Contact 01423 711947/711223

3 *Darley*

The Darley Mill Centre

Located a short drive outside Harrogate is The Darley Mill Centre – a 17th century corn mill which is home to one of the largest working waterwheels in Yorkshire.

For shoppers it's one not to miss and its appeal extends to all ages. The mill houses an impressive selection of linens, crafts and exclusive gifts, with the stone building providing an attractive and complementary backdrop.

Historically this is a place of great interest. According to folklore Darley was the home of famous highwayman Dick Turpin and it is said he held up many a stagecoach nearby. Today the only thing you are likely to find in the middle of the road is a stray sheep!

Sitting on the banks of one of the many streams that feed the River Nidd, the mill used to take grain from the surrounding area for grinding into flour. In 1874 a large iron waterwheel powered it. This 27-foot wheel ceased to work in the 1950s and restoration work by local craftsmen took six months and used five tons of elm and 2,000 nuts and bolts.

A stop here to look at the wheel alone is well worth it, and there is also a collection of original milling machinery to see, a licensed restaurant, tearooms and gardens.

You will doubtless find something to tempt you in either the craft and gift shop or the linen mill shop, which has an ever-changing range of high quality items.

Opening Times The Darley Mill Centre is open every day including Sundays and Bank Holidays. 9.30am to 5.30pm Monday to Saturday, and 11am to 5pm Sunday. It is located seven miles west of Harrogate along the A59 on the outskirts of the village of Darley.

Address Darley, Nidderdale

Contact 01423 780857

Harrogate

Allens of Harrogate

Harrogate would not be the same place without Allens of Harrogate, a family-run fashion business that exudes traditional standards and charm, and has done since it first opened in the town back in 1880.

The shop, with its three floors of fashion for men and ladies and accessories, leather goods, and exclusive gifts, attracts customers from far and wide with its high standards of service and the superior cut and quality of its clothes.

Allens' long history began when William Grover Allen opened his first shop in Parliament Street, Harrogate, in 1880. In 1891 he bought 6 Prospect Crescent for the sum of £2,530.

William's eldest son Bert followed him into the business and later saw the potential to expand the store to provide a sales area on all three floors, which customers still enjoy today.

Following William's death Bert's sons, Jack and Bill, joined the family business and together worked there for over 50 years. Today the business is still in the capable hands of the Allen family with the store being managed by great granddaughters of William, cousins Diana and Liz, with a further cousin, Jane, helping out during busy times.

The unique character of the shop remains, with its mahogany fittings and sweeping staircase as traditional and solid as the service.

Opening Times 9am to 5.30pm Monday to Saturday.

Address 6 Prospect Crescent, Harrogate

Contact 01423 504497 • www.allensofharrogate@fsbdial.co.uk

Bettys Café Tea Room/Taylors of Harrogate

Harrogate is home to Taylors of Harrogate, the family tea and coffee merchants responsible for bringing us Yorkshire Tea – one of the country's top tea brands.

Established in 1886 by Charles Taylor, the name Taylors of Harrogate is renowned far and wide for its superb range of quality products and enjoys a reputation of being one of the country's leading tea and coffee specialists. Its buyers visit tea gardens and coffee estates throughout the world in search of the very best quality teas and unusual and exclusive coffees.

Many years ago Taylors of Harrogate ran a chain of coffee shops known as 'Kiosks' where coffee was freshly roasted in the shop window and customers could relax over a refreshing cup of tea or coffee. These shops enjoyed great success in the years leading up to the Second World War, culminating in the opening of the Café Imperial in Harrogate which served exotic teas from all over the world to the accompaniment of a string quartet. Difficulties arose after the war, however, in keeping the larger cafés open and, in 1962, Taylors joined forces with Bettys Café Tea Rooms.

The rest, as they say, is history, with Taylors of Harrogate and its sister company Bettys enjoying phenomenal success – proving yet again that people appreciate quality and fine food and drink.

Bettys is a Yorkshire tradition of which you cannot nor should not deprive yourself. There are five Bettys Café Tea Rooms in Yorkshire. These can be found in Harrogate, Ilkley, Northallerton and York (where there are two, including the company's smallest shop and café – Little Bettys on Stonegate).

Every time I visit a Bettys Café people can be found queueing patiently for a table while taking the opportunity to savour the traditional English appeal of these elegant establishments. It is like stepping back in time, to a period when courtesies and old-fashioned values reigned and afternoon tea was taken at one's leisure – each mouthful of freshly-baked scone and home-made jam and cream a sheer unadulterated pleasure. This is the appeal of Bettys today. It is the perfect tea room, where you can switch off to the soothing melodies of the piano.

A Swiss confectioner, Frederick Belmont, founded Bettys in 1919, and still, more than 80 years on, the continental connection is much in evidence. Visitors find treats such as Lebkuchen, Biber and continental fancies alongside Yorkshire curd tarts, tea loaves and Fat Rascals.

All the tea rooms have wonderful shops selling a fabulous range of breads, chocolates, biscuits and cakes, as well as an extensive range of teas and coffees.

The shops are entirely self-sufficient. All the breads and cakes – more than 300 lines in all – are make by hand at Bettys Café Bakery in Harrogate. The teas and coffees are specially imported and blended by sister company, Taylors of Harrogate.

Bettys and Taylors' products are available by post or by Internet, so if after visiting you want to remind yourself of your delightful encounter with Bettys access www.bettysbypost.com

Opening Times Bettys Café at Harrogate is open 9am to 9pm seven days a week.

Address 1 Parliament Street, Harrogate

Contact 01423 502746 • www.bettysandtaylors.co.uk

Taylors of Harrogate Pagoda House, Prospect Road, Harrogate

Contact 01423 889822 • www.bettysandtaylors.co.uk

John Cornforth

Like many people I have something of a shoe fetish. This, combined with a distinct dislike of mass-produced items, led to great glee when I discovered John Cornforth at Harrogate.

John's shoes are as far removed from the mass-produced items of footwear as I could ever hope to get. He works very slowly –

making fewer than 30 pairs of shoes a year. His craftsmanship will cost you more than a typical high street pair, but these will not possess the glove-fit or panache of your bespoke shoes.

Prices start at just under £400 and the cost is easily equated with the amount of time and skill that goes into creating these very special shoes.

John has been creating shoes and boots to individual specifications for discerning ladies and gentlemen since 1984. He starts by measuring the customer's feet around all the sensitive points, making extra allowance for irregularities. He then fits up a pair of lasts to match the shape of the feet – so he can make the shoes as broad or as narrow as needed. Patterns are then made using the lasts and materials selected from a wide range of leathers of different shades, textures and finishes – from the finest calf or suede to the softest kid.

After cutting out, the pieces of leather are stitched together and any fancy stitching or decoration done. Leather insoles are fitted to the lasts and the uppers pulled over.

After a couple of days on the lasts, the uppers are sewn to the insoles, the lasts removed and the shoes prepared for a try-on. Getting the right fit may require two or more visits.

Once a customer is happy with the fit, the shoes will be finished and ready to wear within a few days of the final try-on.

It's a wonderful way to get a new pair of shoes, with the bespoke service provided by John allowing you to take an active part in the design and production of your footwear. From choosing the style, through to the selection of leathers, the shape of the toes, and the degree of suppleness or rigidity at key points, you can say exactly what you want.

If you want further pairs it is useful to note that second and subsequent pairs that are made on the same lasts can be ordered and sent to you by post. John also offers a postal repair service.

John's is a very specialised service so be advised of a likely four to eight month waiting period between ordering and completion due to work in progress.

Opening Times Visitors are welcome to call at John's workshop.

Woodlands Avenue is off the A661 Wetherby Road about one mile outside Harrogate centre.

Address 31 Woodlands Avenue, Harrogate

Contact 01423 886928

John Farrah's of Harrogate

The Queen is said to have a liking for it, Selfridges sell it, and people everywhere are hooked on its special taste – of course, it's John Farrah's Original Harrogate Toffee to which I am referring.

The John Farrah name and its distinctive blue and silver tins are known and loved throughout the world, and it is a love affair that began back in 1840 when John Farrah's Original Harrogate Toffee was established.

The toffee was first produced to take away the foul sulphurous taste of the Harrogate spa waters. This is why the toffee is so hard, as it is designed to be long-lasting as opposed to the chewy caramel variety.

It is at the John Farrah Toffee Factory at Starbeck, close to Harrogate, that the secret recipe is used and safeguarded. It is made in open copper pans and stirred with a large wooden paddle.

Since early 1997 the John Farrah company has been owned and run by the Marston family – Gary Marston and wife Jean, and their son Peter. The Marston family home was, ironically, once owned by John Farrah.

Gary originally just had the John Farrah shop in Montpellier Parade, but grasped an opportunity to buy the whole business and the secret toffee recipe when it came up.

Today the company is going from strength to strength. Gary recalls with pride a visit by Her Majesty the Queen to the factory in 1998 to witness the toffee being made.

The John Farrah shop in Harrogate is a honey pot for visitors eager to get a taste of history – quite literally! Its fine selection of toffees, chocolates, fudge, and sweets, and other quality produce is all very tempting. Farrah's now make a fabulous range of their own chocolates too, which are simply delicious.

Farrah's also have two other shops, which are 'The Oldest Chemist Shop in England' at Knaresborough, and another at **Lightwater Valley Shopping Village** at Ripon.

'**The Oldest Chemist Shop in England**' dates back to 1720 and it displays all Farrah's scrumptious products alongside wonderful items such as traditional lavender water and aromatherapy products and fine soaps. At the time of writing plans for a tea-room above the Knaresborough shop were well under way and sounding very appealing. I was also told that a new softer caramel-style Farrah's toffee was imminent, with a red and silver tin.

Farrah's operate a mail order service and a popular hamper-making service.

Opening Times 9am to 5.30pm Monday to Saturday, 10am to 5pm Sunday.

Address 31 Montpellier Parade, Harrogate

Contact 01423 525266 • www.farrahs.com

The Oldest Chemist Shop in England, Market Place, Knaresborough Telephone: 01423 863153

Lightwater Valley Shopping Village, Ripon Telephone: 01765 635471

Ogden of Harrogate Limited

Ogden of Harrogate Limited is a shining example of a Yorkshire family business. It has a fascinating history spanning more than a century and is run today by the great grandson of the founder.

Ogden's sophisticated Edwardian showroom, which lies behind a striking shop façade, offers a collection of antique jewellery that is renowned as without comparison outside London. For those customers with more fashionable tastes, there is also a fine selection of modern jewellery.

The company has its own workshop and its skilled team specialises in designing and hand-making new pieces of jewellery to suit customers' individual requirements. If you have a gemstone, for example, drawings produced by Ogden's resident

designer can be used to create an exquisite setting for it. Existing jewellery can also be remodelled in the workshop.

There is a repair desk, which can mend all varieties of jewellery, watches and silver. It can also handle pearl threading and engraving work. Valuations are a major part of the company's work.

The ethos of the Ogden business, where customers are always treated to a level of service rarely found today, is as integral to its success today as it was in 1893 when James Roberts Ogden founded the company.

The story behind Ogden of Harrogate Limited is a spellbinding one, starting on April 27, 1893, when James Ogden opened his first shop at 23 Cambridge Street, Harrogate. The very first item sold was a hall clock for £2.12.6.

Its long history has included a London branch and several changes of address round Harrogate. It has had many notable sales and commissions over the years. The Harrogate shop, for example, received an order to supply a special cigar box for Churchill.

Another wonderful tale arises from the Coronation of George VI. Ogden's acquired the famous diamond coronet that was created at the command of the Emperor Napoleon for his wife Josephine. It was sold to a lady of title and she wore it at the coronation.

There are endless anecdotes to recount, each one fascinating and all illustrating the wealth of experience and dedication behind this family business.

Today's proprietor Glen Ogden is continuing the business in a manner his great grandfather would have been proud of.

Opening Times 9.15am to 5pm Monday to Saturday.

Address 38 James Street, Harrogate

Contact 01423 504123 • www.ogden-of-harrogate.co.uk

Woods of Harrogate

Established in 1895, Woods of Harrogate epitomises stylish living. For fine linens and interior design there is nowhere better.

A householder's treasure trove, Woods of Harrogate sells exquisite items such as cashmere blankets and appliquéd towels and offers the services of monogramming and other hand embroidery to order that are so rarely found nowadays.

The supreme quality of the shop's stock is no doubt due to the fact that William Woods himself, who is grandson of the shop's founder, has personally approved every single item stocked by Woods.

Mr Woods great-grandfather ran a linen mill in Knaresborough and his son (also William) was prominent in Victorian Harrogate. The previous Princess Royal, who resided at Harewood House, was a devoted Woods' customer until her death and helped to increase its profile.

Today people travel from far and wide to visit this Aladdin's Cave and enjoy some good old fashioned standards of service and attention to detail. Even the opening times ring of a bygone age – the shop is closed at lunchtimes and all weekend.

Opening Times 9am to 1pm and 2.15pm to 5.30pm Monday to Friday.

Address Prince Albert Row, Station Parade, Harrogate

Contact 01423 530111

⑤ *Knaresborough*

Henshaw's Arts and Crafts Centre

I had the great fortune to be given a guided tour of the Henshaw's Arts and Crafts Centre some time ago and I was as impressed then as I am today with its distinctive architecture and the quality of arts and crafts displayed.

The centre was opened in 1998 and provides opportunities in training, education and employment within an arts culture for young adults with a visual impairment. It can accommodate up to 60 young adults at a time in ten modern workshops that offer everything from pottery and sculpture to performing arts and horticulture.

Its facilities are open to the public and a fashionable café gallery stages regular exhibitions by local and other artists. There is also an ongoing programme of workshops and performing arts events for the public.

The centre is located in a walled garden in the grounds of Conyngham Hall and includes two magnificent courtyard areas. One of these is dominated by a wonderful wooden storyteller's throne carved by the well-known sculptor Colin Wilbourn from a 200-year-old oak tree. You simply must have a look at this yourself – it is amazing. The wooden throne combines with a maze and another stunning sculpture to create a magical environment. The area is used for performing arts events and is offered to the community and to schools for performances. During the school holidays the centre runs arts and craft workshops and storytelling sessions for youngsters.

Opening Times 9.30am to 5pm Monday to Friday. Opening at weekends during holiday periods.

Address Bond End, Knaresborough

Contact 01423 541888

•www.knaresborough.co.uk/charities/henshaws

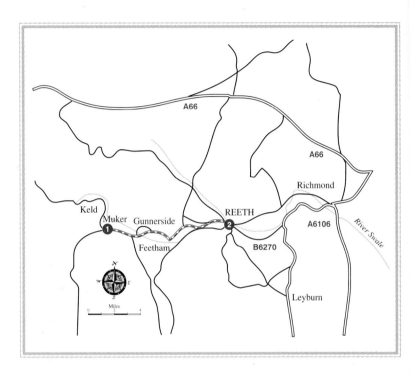

① Muker
Swaledale Woollens

② Reeth
Pete Back
Philip Bastow Cabinetmaker
Clock Works

The Garden House
Hazel Smith Gallery
Pots 'n' Presents
Shades of Heather
Stef's models

Swaledale

Introduction

Swaledale is renowned for its lovely wildflower meadows and unspoiled landscape. It is a great place for walkers, cyclists – and shoppers!

The natural beauty of the area has inspired a number of craftspeople to work here and during a visit you will be able to find many of them engrossed in creating a fascinating range of products – from guitars and pottery to brightly-coloured rag rugs. These are usually sold within the welcoming and, more often than not, busy and cluttered environment of their workshops.

This trail centres largely on the pretty village of Reeth, a haven for craft folk, and full of shopping finds for the visitor including self-taught guitar maker Pete Back, the colourful material-strewn garden studio of rag rug maker Heather Ritchie, and the workshop of Stef's Models.

You may also like to learn about the crafts of the past in this area at the Swaledale Folk Museum at Reeth.

It is easy to see why artists Thomas Girtin and J M W Turner made painting expeditions to the area. It is a place which inspires much creativity, both then and now.

Muker

Swaledale Woollens Limited

Knitting is a fast-declining craft in today's world of mass-produced garments, but thankfully it is still possible to find quality hand-knitted items in some shops – including the cottage shop of Swaledale Woollens Limited in the lovely village of Muker.

For over a quarter of a century Swaledale Woollens has been producing quality knitwear using wool mostly from the Swaledale sheep, but also using other British speciality wools. Its team of talented local knitters, many working in their own homes, creates a fabulous range of garments, including sweaters, cardigans, gloves, hats and even hand-knitted socks.

At the cottage shop in Muker you can view all the styles of garments and also learn more about sheep and the Swaledale breed, together with the history of wool and knitting.

Swaledale Woollens has a worldwide reputation and regularly sends items to America and Japan.

Opening Times The shop is open Monday to Saturday 10am until 5.30pm, and Sunday 10am until 5.30pm (5pm in winter). It is closed Mondays mid January to mid March.

Address Strawbeck, Muker. Muker is 20 miles west of Richmond and six miles from Hawes.

Contact 01748 886251 •
www.yorkshirenet.co.uk/swaledalewoollens

Reeth

Pete Back

Sadly, I cannot profess to be very musical. What I do have, however, is an appreciation of fine musical instruments and discovering guitar maker Pete Back in the village of Reeth and his superb range of hand-built guitars was a real joy.

Pete's is a fascinating story. He is a self-taught craftsman who started out making guitars after using one belonging to his son as a template. At the time he worked in a coal-mining engineering department and had to go down the pit once a week to examine machinery. He managed to get some mahogany from some very old mine workings and retreated into his small shed with the wood and his son's guitar. He made the body of the instrument and later completed it after buying a new guitar and cutting its neck to see the truss rod and how it was fitted.

He kept the first guitar he made, but the second was bought by a shop in Rotherham for £50. The same shop bought his third and fourth guitars and things started to snowball. Pete gave up his job and took up guitar making for a living.

He once took some of his guitars to the City Hall at Sheffield to let the bands playing there see what they thought of them. Thin Lizzy was on and the band members were very impressed with the guitars and Pete got two orders.

Prices range from £600 upward and Pete makes most types to order.

At his Reeth showroom you can view, and play if you wish, his range of electric, folk and classical guitars, which form a stunning display.

Opening Times 10am to 6pm most days all year round.

Address 8 Silver Street, Reeth

Contact 01748 884887 • www.guitarmaker.co.uk

Philip Bastow – Cabinetmaker

The smell of newly cut and planed wood greets the nostrils when you enter the Reeth workshop of cabinetmaker Philip Bastow. Here you can both see Philip hard at work in the sawdust-strewn interior and view impressive examples of completed pieces of furniture and gifts in wood.

Philip specialises in the design and manufacture of individual furniture commissions, using mainly oak, ash, elm and sycamore. He also carries out specialist joinery and produces a gift range that includes bookends, breadboards, candlesticks, stools, and small occasional tables.

Philip welcomes people to pop in and have a browse round.

Opening Times 9am to 5pm Monday to Friday, 9am to 12 noon Saturday, Sundays and evening visits by appointment.

Address Reeth Dales Centre, Silver Street, Reeth

Contact 01748 884555

Clock Works

Ian Whitworth is a man with time on his hands, so to speak, but none to spare. For Ian owns Clock Works at Reeth where a stunning range of clocks and barometers are designed and handcrafted. These include a Classical Grandfather Clock design and a 'Black Forest' Wall Clock.

Ian started Clock Works in 1994 to produce, repair and restore clocks and barometers. He initially worked from home, but in 1997 when the business outgrew his home workshop he moved to the Reeth Dales Centre.

A newly extended showroom area at Clock Works displays a full range of the clocks and barometers now designed and made. All are beautiful objects and include the Millennium Bracket Clock which features a secret compartment or 'time capsule' built into the case where family history details or photographs can be placed as a record of the present day, for future generations to discover.

Ian, a member of the British Watch and Clockmakers Guild, continues to repair and restore clocks and barometers that are brought to him for attention from far and wide.

Opening Times Clock Works is open Tuesday to Friday 10.30am to 5pm and Saturday 10.30am to 12.30pm. Telephone for Bank Holiday opening times.

Address Reeth Dales Centre, Silver Street, Reeth

Contact 01748 884088 • www.clockmakers.co.uk

The Garden House

This delightful little shop is tucked sneakily away in the corner of Anvil Square and is well worth seeking out. Here you will discover the work of potters Ray and Jane Davies and also a range of work by other skilled local craftspeople in wood, paper, cloth, wool and clay.

The charming building, which was once an old field barn and then a smithy, forms the perfect setting for such a shop and is brimming with character.

There are lots of exclusive designs and novel gifts to be found here, the main draw being the pottery made by the owners. This is made at a pottery workshop on The Green at Reeth. Using a wide range of clays, Ray and Jane make pots for the garden and the house in high-fired stoneware and terracotta. Their range includes planters, wall plant pockets, hanging baskets, seed trays, plant labels, flowerpots, decorative wall plaques, and house name and number plaques in frost-proof stoneware.

The couple's work is all individually handcrafted and their distinctive style is the result of a deep love of gardens and plants.

Opening Times The Garden House Shop is open from April to October every day but Wednesday 10am to 5.30pm, and from October to the end of December on Friday, Saturday and Sunday 10.30am to 4pm. The shop is closed in January to the end of March except by appointment. The Garden House Pottery workshop is open by appointment only.

Address Anvil Square, Reeth

Contact 01748 884188

Hazel Smith Gallery

Local scenes captured on canvas in paint and pastels by artists Hazel and Vic Smith can be seen at the Hazel Smith Gallery.

These original works are available only through this small and friendly gallery and offer you the chance to purchase the work of two talented local artists at affordable prices. Many people return after a first purchase.

Opening Times 11am to 4pm Tuesday to Saturday. Closed Sunday and Monday.

Address The Dales Centre, Reeth

Contact 01748 884663

Pots 'n' Presents

Exclusive pottery is available at this shop close to The Black Bull. It is all hand-thrown and hand-finished and offers an extensive range at affordable prices. There is also a large range of silver jewellery and other gifts.

Opening Times 10am to 5.30pm, Monday to Saturday. Closed Sunday.

Address Anvil Square, Reeth

Contact 01748 884687

Shades of Heather

Rag rug maker and teacher Heather Ritchie has a dream studio located in her garden, which looks out both onto her country cottage garden and to the fields beyond. The workshop is a feast of colour and texture and brimming with work at various stages of being crafted. Some of this work is still waiting patiently to be completed years after being started because its maker is always so busy, doing commissions or teaching the various methods of rag rug making to groups eager to master this traditional craft.

Historically Swaledale was one of the principal areas for rag rug making. Miners' stone-built cottages in the region had flagged floors and these were adorned with 'clippy' and 'hooky' mats made from old clothing and lisle stockings.

The rugs were traditionally worked on recycled sacks and were limited in terms of colour. Today design opportunities for rag rug making are endless with so many colourful materials available.

Keen to keep this old craft alive, Heather teaches rag rug making at her studio and sells all that you need to do the craft. Here you can buy kits, wools, fabrics, dyed swatches, backing fabrics, hessians, cutting boards and dyes. A mail order service is also available.

Heather runs both daily and longer residential workshops, offering

accommodation to those attending in her home.

She says the workshops are great fun and suitable for beginners upwards. I quite fancy having a go myself. The thought of spending a few days here in the beautiful village of Reeth learning an age-old craft has a strong appeal.

Heather's husband Les crafts rag rug-making tools. These include a range of fabulous hand turned hooks in exotic hard woods from sustainable forests and rag rug frames.

Heather takes commissions for both rag rugs and wall hangings, done in 'proddy' and 'hooky'.

Opening Times It is advisable to telephone before visiting.

Address The Garden Rug Studio, Greencroft, Reeth

Contact 01748 884435 • www.rugmaker.clara.net

Stef's models

I remember the look of delight on my late grandfather's face when I gave him a model of a sheepdog for what was to be his last birthday. He had a deep love for the breed and a constant real-life sheepdog companion for many a happy year.

The model I gave as a gift was in fact one created at Stef's at Reeth, the birthplace of many much-treasured and collected sculptured animal figures and wall plaques.

This thriving business centres on Stef Ottevanger, who has had a keen interest in making sculptures of animals since childhood. She developed the interest after a fine arts course at Harrogate College of Art and a career teaching, and in the early 1980s started to make clay sculptures of domestic animals. Initially this was a hobby, but a number of commissions then followed and she subsequently began trading as 'Stef's Models'.

Stef designed a range of farm animal figures and produced her own moulds from these. To start with production took place in her home and the kitchen was transformed into a factory each morning. Later, the workshop was set up at Reeth and a small team employed to carry out casting, mould making and hand painting for an ever increasing number of products.

Stef's models are now sold all over the world, but they all start their lives at the Reeth Dales Centre.

All the designs are made by Stef, who draws her inspiration from the surrounding Dales countryside. The processes of mould making, casting, hand painting and finishing all take place at the Reeth workshop and visitors are welcome to watch all the stages.

Many visitors have become avid collectors and are eager to see the new releases on their regular visits to Stef's, or hear about them in the 'collectors' newsletters.

Stef's range now numbers over 200 items and includes dogs, sheep, cattle, ponies, farmyard animals, wildlife, and a distinctive collection of wall plaques.

Stef also does commissions, which are stunning in their detail and likeness to their subject/s.

Opening Times 9am to 4pm Monday to Friday year round, 10am to 4pm Saturday, 11am – 4pm Sunday and Bank Holidays between Easter and the end of October.

Address Reeth Dales Centre, Silver Street, Reeth

Contact 01748 884498

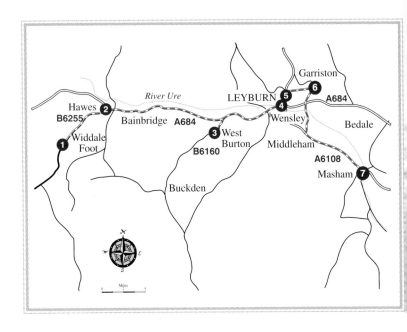

1 Widdale Foot
Wensleydale Rocking Horses

2 Hawes
Outhwaite Ropemakers
Wensleydale Creamery
Wensleydale Pottery

3 West Burton
The Cat Pottery

4 Wensley
White Rose Candles

5 Leyburn
The Teapottery

6 Garriston
Wensleydale Longwool Sheepshop

7 Masham
Black Sheep Brewery
Black Bull in Paradise Visitor Centre
(Theakston's Brewery)
Island Heritage Rare Breeds Wool

Wensleydale

Introduction

Wensleydale is a lush valley famous for its waterfalls – especially Hardraw and Aysgarth – its wonderful barn and drystone wall landscape and, of course, its cheese!

There is no end to the shopping opportunities here – from exquisite hand-crafted rocking horses that have a timeless appeal (whether you are eight or eighty), to candles, pottery and rope. If you like to buy something very individual and also enjoy watching it being created then this area will be a real treat. There is a veritable feast of intriguing shops and workshops for you to visit.

You will love the shop-lined cobbled streets of the market towns of Hawes, Leyburn and Masham. At Hawes there is an array of things to see, including the home of Wensleydale Cheese – a great favourite with Wallace and Gromit. At the Wensleydale Creamery Visitor Centre you can learn all about the history of the loveable duo's favourite snack in the museum and see real Wensleydale Cheese being made in the dairy.

Just a short drive from Hawes you will find the picturesque home of young Wensleydale craftsman James Ogden and wonder at his beautiful hand-carved rocking horses.

Further east in Leyburn you will be amazed at the range of fabulous teapots produced at The Teapottery, and any cat lover will find The Cat Pottery at West Burton a delight.

And if you feel like you need a drink after all that shopping there is always Masham and its two breweries with visitor centres!

A visit to Askrigg is a must for any devotees of *All Creatures Great and Small* – the village was featured in the popular television series.

1 *Widdale Foot*

Wensleydale Rocking Horses

Your journey along the winding Dales roads leading to The Dairy Farm could have no better end than the sight of James Ogden's stunning hand-carved rocking horses.

The idyllic setting is the perfect backdrop for James and his craft. The quality of his work is unmistakable and is the reason for James' fast-growing reputation as both a maker and restorer of hand-carved rocking horses.

Like many a craftsman his work is spread throughout the house with new rocking horses created in one room, old ones being restored in another, and others awaiting attention elsewhere.

At the time of writing Wensleydale Rocking Horses are in the process of converting a barn into a showroom, where visitors will better be able to view some of James' creations.

His rocking horses are fashioned and carved in very much the same way they have been for centuries. They are made mainly from American poplar wood (Tulip wood) due to its strength and

the fact it is a crop wood, although James has made commissioned horses from oak, cherry and walnut.

The horses can be painted or polished and if you choose to buy one you can have a say in colours of paint, leather work and hair. James makes all the leather work on the horses himself, including the saddle, tack and bridle, and can personalise a horse for you with some extra special detailing such as your initials on the bridle. The horses are mounted on ash safety stands, although can be made on bow rockers if preferred.

A former sculptor, James trained in the craft of making rocking horses for six years before striking out on his own. Each horse takes 40 to 45 hours to make, with a lot of waiting and drying in between, and he does absolutely everything himself.

Wensleydale Rocking Horses is located at Widdale Foot, on the road from Hawes to Ingleton.

Opening Times James welcomes people keen to look round the workshop and watch him at his craft.

Address The Dairy Farm, Widdale Foot, Hawes.

Contact 01969 667070

 *Hawes*

Outhwaite Ropemakers

Ropemaking has been a feature of life in the Hawes area for centuries and today provides a thriving business for former college lecturers Peter and Ruth Annison, the owners of Outhwaite Ropemakers.

The couple bought the business from Tom Outhwaite in 1975, agreeing to continue to trade under the long-established name of W R Outhwaite and Son. The Outhwaite family had run the ropemaking business since 1905, after buying it from the original owners, the Wharton family. Census returns for 1841 show Thomas Wharton and his sons John and Richard listed as ropemakers.

Outhwaite Ropemakers has a fascinating history and attracts thousands of visitors every year keen to learn more about this centuries-old craft. For at the Town Foot premises you can not only view and buy finished items made from rope, but also see every stage of the ropemaking process. You can watch as many thin strands of yarn are rapidly twisted into a strong piece of rope.

All manner of items are made today at the ropemakers. Rope can be made up to 100ft long, but most are relatively short. An electric motor-driven ropemaking machine has speeded things up from the old days, but not essentially altered the traditional method of making rope. A hand-powered machine resembling a large spinning wheel was used of old and the last such wheel to be used in Hawes can now be seen at the Upper Dales Folk Museum near to the ropeworks.

Most of the products made at the Hawes ropemakers were traditionally for agricultural use, such as animal halters and cow bands for tethering cattle. Today, however, there is an expansive range of products, including bannister ropes, church bell ropes and an endless selection of dog leads.

The business has come a long way since the day when W R Outhwaite took 3s.9d (18.5 pence) during his first Tuesday's trading at Hawes market, but it still retains all the original appeal of a true traditional Yorkshire craft company.

Opening Times Monday to Friday 9am to 5.30pm (except Christmas and Good Friday), July to October open Saturdays 10am – 5pm.

Address Town Foot, Hawes

Contact 01969 667487 • www.ropemakers.co.uk

Wensleydale Creamery Visitor Centre

I remember many years ago screwing my nose up at my late grandfather when he ate Wensleydale cheese with his apple pie and declaring him rather silly for liking such a strange combination – preferring instead my ice cream accompaniment. Now I know better, however, and he would be pleased to know I'm acquiring his good taste in my old age! He would also be pleased to hear of the continuing and growing success of the

Wensleydale Creamery at Hawes, where delicious, crumbly Wensleydale cheese is produced from Wensleydale milk.

At the Wensleydale Creamery Visitor Centre you can learn all about Wensleydale cheese and, from a viewing gallery, see it being made in the dairy.

The Creamery is known far and wide for its superb range of quality cheeses and it is fascinating to learn the history behind the creamery and its delicious products.

The first recorded origins of Wensleydale cheese go way back in history to 1150 when a monastery was built just outside Hawes. A few years later the monks moved to Jervaulx in Lower Wensleydale where the cheese was made until the dissolution of the monasteries in the 16th century. The cheesemaking art passed from the monks to local farmers' wives, who produced cheese in their farmhouses for around 300 years.

In 1897 a corn and provision merchant from Hawes, Edward Chapman, began to buy milk from surrounding farms and use it for the manufacture of Wensleydale cheese on a larger scale. When the dairy faced closure, Kit Calvert championed the cause of a group of local farmers and they took on the dairy with Kit as the managing director.

Business thrived and in 1953 Kit built a new Wensleydale creamery in Hawes for £15,000, and the same year he re-introduced a miniature 1lb cheese – the 'Baby Wensleydale'. This proved a real hit and by the 1960s sales had reached 250,000 per year.

The Milk Marketing Board bought the creamery in 1966, with Kit staying on to run it until 1967 when he retired. His dedication to the cause of Wensleydale cheese was acknowledged with an MBE in 1977.

The creamery was closed in May 1992 amid public outrage and uproar but was saved by a team of ex-managers, who with the help of a group of former creamery workers recommenced cheese-making at the creamery in December 1992. Eighteen months later the Visitor Centre, with viewing gallery, museum and restaurant, opened its doors to the public.

A visit will furnish you with everything you ever wanted to know about the craft of cheesemaking. I remember watching my mum making cheese many years ago and found the whole process fascinating then – if somewhat time consuming.

There is a wonderful cheese shop at the Visitor Centre, where you can sample different Wensleydale cheeses before buying. Choose from traditional Wensleydale, Mature Wensleydale, Blue Wensleydale, or Wensleydales flavoured with added ginger or apricots, or onions and chives. There are also smoked varieties that are cured in the creamery's own kiln, including Oak-Smoked Traditional and Smoked Blue.

The shop also stocks traditional cheeses from all over the country, together with locally-cured bacon, rich fruit cakes and honey roast sausages made from pigs fed on the creamery's own whey.

There is a gift shop at the Visitor Centre too.

Opening Times Daily 9.30am to 5pm. Optimum viewing time: 10.30am to 2.30pm.

Address Gayle Lane, Hawes

Contact 01969 667664 • www.wensleydale.co.uk

Wensleydale Pottery

As you are strolling round the centre of Hawes you should pay a visit to the Wensleydale Pottery, where you can see potter Simon Shaw at work.

The pottery has been in Hawes since 1983 and Simon produces an attractive range of usable domestic tableware and also promotional items. There is a showroom attached to his workshop for you to browse round.

The pottery is located next door to Kit Calvert's Antiquarian Book Shop, which is well worth a look. (This is the same Kit Calvert who played such an important role in the history of Wensleydale Creamery.)

Opening Times The Wensleydale Pottery is open Monday to Saturday, 10am until 5.30pm.

Address Market Place, Hawes

Contact 01969 667594

③ *West Burton*

The Cat Pottery

This is a heavenly find for all feline-lovers. Located in the beautiful village of West Burton is Moorside Design and during a walk to the workshop you will be welcomed by its cat sculptures among the alpine gardens, enjoying a snooze in the grass, perched on the roofs, or half-hidden beneath the bushes.

Since 1982 Moorside Design, run by Shirley and Barrie Nichols and daughter Sarah, have been producing a range of ceramic cats at The Cat Pottery. Their own cats Chloe, Orlando and Blue have been the models for their work.

Both Sarah and Shirley studied sculpture: Sarah at Edinburgh College of Art, and Shirley at Leeds and the Slade School, London University. Their training and over 18 years shared experience of sculpturing cats allows them to create models that are finely observed and full of character.

Thousands of people visit the workshop each year, many returning time and time again to add to their Moorside Design cat collection.

The Cat Pottery also produces a range of outdoor, life-sized 'stone' cats for the garden and patio, like those displayed outside the workshop.

Opening Times Monday to Friday 9am to 5pm, Saturday and Sunday 10am to 2pm.

Address Moorside Design, West Burton

Contact 01969 663273 • www.catpottery.co.uk

 *Wensley*

White Rose Candles

The wonderful old watermill that is home to White Rose Candles merits a visit in its own right – records show the site of the mill dates back to 1203. However, when such history is combined with a charming candlemaking workshop inside there is even more reason to visit here.

White Rose Candles is run by Mick and Jen White, who set up the business in 1971 at Pudsey. Six years later they moved to Wensley Mill, where they hand-make a wide range of fabulous candles using either traditional dipping techniques or more modern casting methods.

Not only do the couple make nearly all the candles they sell, Mick designs and makes the candlemaking machinery they use from scrap metal and materials.

White Rose Candles specialises in good quality, long lasting candles that don't drip or smoke and have many regular customers who buy their candles over and over again. Their extensive range includes aromatherapy and church candles.

During a visit you can observe the various processes involved in candle manufacture and browse round the shop.

Opening Times Daily except Wednesday and Saturday 10am to 5pm June to November plus holidays. Also Easter and half term. Other times ring for appointment.

Address Wensley Mill, Wensley

Contact 01969 623544

www.yorkshirenet.co.uk/ydales/workshoptrail/index

5 *Leyburn*

The Teapottery

When you visit The Teapottery at Leyburn you will at once discover the truth behind their slogan 'Teatime will never be the same again'. For here you will find the most amazing collection of teapots I suspect you are likely to find anywhere. These are no ordinary teapots – there is nothing faintly resembling what I would usually expect to pour tea out of among the vast collection on show.

For what The Teapottery designs and produces are witty and original teapots that are now collected the world over and their offbeat designs have been spotted in many television shows, films and even pop videos.

Not only can you view the finished teapots here, you can also witness the entire production process and, surprise, surprise, enjoy a lovely cup of tea! For the teapot making factory is open to the public and a special walkway takes you round every stage of production. The Teapottery create all their own designs and each miniature work of art is cast and decorated entirely by hand.

The Teapottery story goes back to 1967 when Martin Bibby and Judy Rance (now Bibby) met at Hornsey College of Art in London. In 1978 they started their own pottery at Swineside in the Yorkshire Dales called 'Swineside Ceramics'. Their early range of products included a set of three teapots and things snowballed from there. They moved the business to Leyburn and their teapots were generating so much interest that they decided to concentrate exclusively on them.

Now based at the purpose-built factory on the Leyburn Business Park, The Teapottery is doing a booming trade. In 1995 a second Teapottery was opened in Keswick in the Lake District. Due to the number of enquiries they receive from collectors they have brought out an annual mail order catalogue.

Martin and Judy still come up with all the captivating designs themselves and have been commissioned to make special teapots by various companies, including Aga-Rayburn. They also do a range of limited edition teapots.

The Teapottery will enchant you with its wonderful array of eccentric designs.

Opening Times 9am to 5pm seven days a week, all year round. Except Christmas Day, Boxing Day and New Year's Day.

Address Leyburn Business Park, Leyburn

Contact 01969 623839

 *Garriston*

Wensleydale Longwool Sheepshop

A short drive from Leyburn you will find the Wensleydale Longwool Sheepshop tucked away behind a farmhouse. The journey will be well rewarded if you appreciate good quality knitwear and knitting yarns.

The Wensleydale sheep is widely acclaimed as the producer of the world's finest lustre longwool and this delightful little shop is renowned for the quality of the wool it produces from the fleece of this rare breed. Its exclusive collection of yarns has twice won the British Wool Marketing Board International Quality Award for its finish, handle and subtle colour range.

The shop was established in 1989 and has grown considerably since then, now exporting to Europe, Australia and America.

The range of products available include hand-knitting yarns commission spun for the shop in Aran, double knitting and four ply, in both natural and a spectrum of gentle country shades. You can also get a wide range of sheepshop hand knitting patterns here that have been specially designed to complement the yarn.

There is a collection of knitwear, hand knitted in the Dales, and fleeces and combed tops for spinners and craft enthusiasts.

Opening Times From April 1 to October 31, Tuesday to Saturday 10am to 5pm, and Bank Holiday Mondays. From November 1, Tuesday only. Other times by appointment.

Address Cross Lanes Farm, Garriston, Leyburn

Contact 01969 623840 • www.lineone.net/-sheepshop

 **7** *Masham*

Black Sheep Brewery Visitor Centre

Smell those hops. You certainly will when you visit the Black Sheep Brewery Visitor Centre at Masham.

The Black Sheep Brewery is an independent, traditional brewer of fine Yorkshire ales and at its Visitor Centre you can experience the brewing process first-hand on a 'shepherded' tour, enjoying a glass of traditionally brewed beer.

For all keen shoppers, there is the Black Sheep Shop. Here you can buy a wide variety of products, from Black Sheep clothing to cuddly sheep, and, of course, beer.

The Black Sheep Brewery was set up in Masham by Paul Theakston, the fifth generation of Masham's famous brewing family. The brewery's first barrels of beer were delivered in October 1992

and it has gone from strength to strength ever since.

I doubt anyone would refer to the brewery as 'new', for the vessels, plant and brewing methods used here are from a bygone age and the building itself is part of the former Lightfoot Brewery. This was Masham's other brewery before Paul's grandfather took it over in 1919.

Opening Times Seven days a week. Sunday and Monday 10am to 5.30pm and Tuesday to Saturday from 10am to 11pm.

Contact 01756 680100 • www.blacksheep.co.uk

'The Black Bull in Paradise' Visitor Centre

In 1827 Robert Theakston took a lease on the Black Bull Inn and brewhouse in Masham – and so the story of Theakston's Brewery begins. In 1875 his son Thomas built the 'new' brewery that stands today on Masham's Paradise Field. Hence the name of the visitor centre.

Theakston's Brewery has a long history of producing quality beers and although it has grown considerably has always kept its roots firmly embedded at Masham.

At the visitor centre you can follow the entire brewing process, from blending the ingredients, through filling the casks, to the craft of the cooper as straight pieces of oak are formed into curved staves to create a sublime vessel that holds a precise measure of beer. If you take a guided tour your thirsty work will be rewarded with a free pint.

Items on sale at the centre include hand-crafted pens, made from oak staves of old Theakston casks.

Opening Times Open every day from April 1st to November 5th. From November 6th to December 12th, open Wednesday, Saturday and Sunday. Opening times: 10.30am to 5.30pm.

Address Theakston's Brewery, Masham

Contact 01765 680000 • www.theakstons.co.uk

Island Heritage (Rare Breeds Wool)

A truly beautiful collection of clothes and accessories is to be found at Island Heritage (Rare Breeds Wool) just a few miles from Masham, made from the undyed wools of rare breed, primitive sheep.

This is a working dales farm where the sheep bred not only play an important role in a programme of conservation supported by the Rare Breeds Survival Trust, but have also been chosen for the rich and varied colour and lustre of their fleeces. These include the Hebridean, Manx Loghtan, North Ronaldsay and Shetland.

Island Heritage's own fleeces and those from a number of other Primitive Sheep breeders are carefully sorted for colour and type by expert wool graders before being spun to their specification by a specialist spinner. The yarns are then woven into fabrics to Island Heritage's own designs by experienced local weavers, and hand-tailored and crafted into an exclusive range of clothes and accessories. The yarns are also hand-knitted or hand-framed into distinctive garments.

You will find much to tempt you, with a full range for men and women, and soft furnishings too. The collection, which features coats, waistcoats, skirts, trousers, cardigans, jumpers, shawls, and much more, incorporates both modern and traditional styles and is exclusive to Island Heritage.

Attached to the shop is a workroom where you can see some of the goods being made up, and, as it is a working farm, you can enjoy seeing the sheep in the surrounding fields.

Opening Times April to the end of October: Tuesday to Sunday 10am to 6pm, closed Monday except Bank Holiday; November to the end of March: All week 11am to 4pm; closed Christmas Eve to Boxing Day, January and February. A good idea to phone first.

Address Pott Hall Farm, Near Leighton Reservoir, Healey, Masham

Contact 01765 689651 • www.islandheritage.co.uk

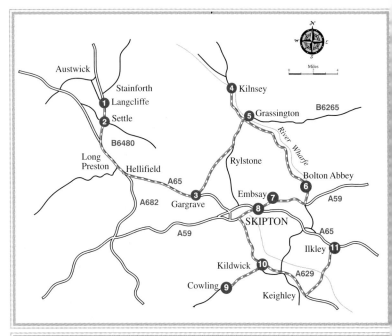

1 Langcliffe
Watershed Mill

2 Settle
Dugdales
Mary Milnthorpe and Daughters
Benjamin Thomas

3 Gargrave
Dorothy Ward

4 Kilnsey
Kilnsey Park and Trout Farm

5 Grassington
Martyn Fretwell
Gemini Studios

6 Bolton Abbey
Bolton Abbey Iron-Art

7 Embsay
Embsay Needlecraft Centre

8 Skipton
Avena Herbal Products
Stanforths pork pies
Whitakers chocolates

9 Cowling
Brent Gallery

10 Kildwick
Spinning Jenny

11 Ilkley
Humphreys
David Lishman Butchers

The Southern Dales

Introduction

I have to confess a strong natural bias to this particular part of Yorkshire. I was lucky enough to be brought up in Giggleswick and to spend the first six years of my working life as a reporter on the *Craven Herald and Pioneer* newspaper at Skipton.

Settle is a charming market town with endless character and appeal where my family has a long-established shop, Dugdales, where I help out on occasion! The town offers a wide choice of shops and is also home to Watershed Mill and The Dalesmade Centre, where you can buy an impressive range of quality, locally-produced crafts. The town is also the starting point of the Settle-Carlisle Railway, which provides a breathtaking journey over the Ribblehead Viaduct.

Wharfedale is a beautiful place and visitors can enjoy a visit to Kilnsey Park and Trout Farm, just a short distance from the dramatic Kilnsey Crag and the fields used for the annual Kilnsey Show.

Grassington exudes charm with its cobbled streets and small, individual shops. Malham is a real must – this is a wonderful village and home to some breathtaking limestone features, the most impressive of which is Malham Cove.

The historic market town of Skipton has much to commend it, including Whitakers chocolates and wonderful cheeses sold on its outdoor market.

Bolton Abbey is a popular beauty spot. You can rest those shopping-weary legs for a while on the banks of the River Wharfe and enjoy the spectacle of Bolton Priory.

Only a few miles away is Ilkley, a very classy town with tree-lined shopping streets and its own Bettys Café. It's a must for clothes shopping and also has an excellent selection of fine restaurants.

❶ *Langcliffe*

Watershed Mill Visitor Centre

This former 1820's cotton mill situated on the banks of the River Ribble is now a Visitor Centre offering endless shopping opportunities.

For not only is the former mill home to The Edinburgh Woollen Mill, it also features The Dalesmade Centre which displays over 40 Dales crafts. These include woodwork, pottery, leatherwork, paintings, prints and textiles – all made by talented local craftspeople.

Bentham Pottery's highly collectable work and the superb batik designs of Jill James from Austwick can be seen here, alongside the work of Pateley Bridge glassmakers Sanders and Wallace and Bradley aviation and transport artist David R Watson. Beautiful ranges of hand-painted silk products are available from Christine Carradice and Jill Clay, there are photographs of Yorkshire landscape from David Green,

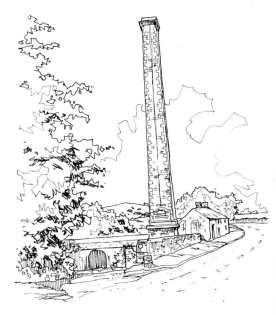

and more stunning photographs of the Dales from Keld Crafts, of Leyburn – plus lots, lots more.

There is also a rock and fossil shop, and a coffee shop serving home-baked Dales food.

Opening Times 10am to 5.30pm Monday to Saturday, 11am to 5pm Sunday. Closed Christmas Day and Easter Sunday.

Address Watershed Mill, Langcliffe Road, Settle

Contact 01729 825539/825111

 Settle

Dugdales

I should never be forgiven if I omitted Dugdales, which is such an integral part of my family's heritage. Founded by my great grandfather William Eddy Dugdale in 1906 it passed on to my grandfather Tom Dugdale and is now run today by my parents Ian and Barbara Johnson.

It is an electrical and agricultural business, serving farmers from Lancaster to Harrogate and the wider local community and in essence has not changed a great deal since the days I remember helping my grandfather in the shop as a young child. My two daughters now enjoy helping (or is that hinder mum and dad?), their nana and grandad, today.

For visitors it provides a rare opportunity to see what is still essentially an old-fashioned shop that has a charm all of its own. Here you will find items no high street outlet will furnish you with, including hay rakes, walking sticks, scythes, milk cans, hen feeders, dog whistles and locally made garden furniture.

A lack of sophistication and the upholding of traditional values carried through the generations make Dugdales a rare find. The Settle shop, with its concrete floor, is also the coolest place to seek refuge on a hot summer's day!

Dugdales also has another shop at Skipton Auction Mart.

Opening Times The Settle shop is open 8.30am to 5pm Monday to Friday and 8.30am to 12.30pm Saturday.

Address Kirkgate, Settle

Contact 01729 822337

Mary Milnthorpe and Daughters

For anyone with an interest in antique silver and jewellery this shop is a must. My treasured engagement ring was bought here and every time I visit I am bewildered by the choice of quality goods. It is no wonder people travel many miles to visit this family-run shop.

There has been a jewellery/watchmaking business at the premises since the property was built in 1812. The present owners are the great-granddaughters of the jeweller who had the business in 1900.

Opening Times Closed Sunday and Wednesday. Open other days: 9.30am to 12.30pm and 1.45pm to 5pm.

Address The Antique Shop, Market Place, Settle

Contact 01729 822331

Benjamin Thomas Woodwork

Here at Benjamin Thomas Woodwork you can view some lovely hand-made furniture in red wood, pitch pine and hardwood that is made on the premises. The showroom also displays antiques and reconditioned furniture and a range of arts and crafts.

Opening Times Closed Sunday and Monday.

Address 2 Chapel Street, Settle

Contact 01729 822760 • www.btwoodwork.co.uk

 *Gargrave*

Dorothy Ward

If you are looking for a special gift a visit to Dorothy Ward at Gargrave, which has now been trading for half a century, is sure to furnish you with just that.

Located in a converted barn, this lovely shop is home to an Aladdin's Cave of quality gifts that are that little bit different, including knitwear, crystal, wooden toys, and basketware.

The barn was converted by Dorothy and Nig Gledhill and Dorothy's mother, also Dorothy, in 1966/67 and is now run by Stuart Gledhill, who is third generation, and his wife Maria. Helped by a small team they provide a very personal, friendly service and always gift wrap everything beautifully!

Opening Times 9am to 5.30pm Monday to Saturday. Closed Sunday.

Address The Barn, North Street, Gargrave

Contact 01756 749275

 *Kilnsey*

Kilnsey Park and Trout Farm

A short distance from the impressive outcrop of limestone that is Kilnsey Crag you will find Kilnsey Park and Trout Farm, a place with no shortage of attractions and opportunities for visitors. There is fly fishing, children's fun fishing, radio controlled boats, trout viewing and feeding areas, a conservation and nature trail, children's adventure playground, a specialist herb and alpine centre, and more besides.

Kilnsey Park has been established as a trout farm for over 16 years and now features a tearoom/restaurant that seats 50 people, and a delicatessen shop. The shop produce is based on rainbow trout from the farm – smoked pâtés, smoked trout with honey and mustard, cold smoked trout, terrines, smoked trout pancakes and fish dishes prepared by their own chef, smokies, peppered fillets, fresh trout and fillets etc. There are approximately 16 different trout products for sale.

The shop also sells local cheeses, unusual jams, jellies, mustards and chutneys and a wide variety of game from their own estate.

Opening Times 9am to 5.30pm all year round.

Address Kilnsey near Skipton

Contact 01756 752150

⑤ *Grassington*

Martyn Fretwell

A former blacksmith's forge, dating back to the early 1600's, provides a historic setting for the oil paintings of landscape artist Martyn Fretwell.

Martyn, a former art teacher, bought a property in Hebden in 1982 to use as a weekend retreat from his teaching career. In 1989 it became his permanent home and in 1993 he opened the Shenstone Gallery at 39 Main Street, Grassington. Here you can see his landscape paintings of the Dales, mainly Wharfedale, and often catch him at work.

He used to concentrate on portrait work, in pastels, but now enjoys giving real depth to a Dales landscape painting using the glorious textures and effects that oils create.

Visitors buy a large proportion of his paintings and he often sends his work to customers overseas. He says he loves painting the Wharfedale area because it offers so much variety in its landscape.

What is refreshing for the visitor is that Martyn is always at the gallery, allowing you to chat with the artist in person.

As well as many original works there are also prints and limited editions for sale.

Opening Times 9.30am to 5pm Monday, Tuesday and Thursday. 9.30am to 5.30pm Friday, Saturday and Sunday.

Address Shenstone Gallery, 39 Main Street, Grassington

Contact 01756 752692/752120

Gemini Studios

Gemini Studios is the shop of Sheila Denby and Daughters. Now I remember Sheila Denby, a journalist herself, often popping into the *Craven Herald* during my time as a reporter there with articles of local interest and stopping a while to chat. She is a lovely lady, who not only writes and is the parish council clerk at

Grassington (a post she has held for three decades!), but also runs this wonderful shop in the village with help from her daughters Jane, Katie and Joanna.

Gemini Studios has been established for 16 years and is located in a lovely 17th century barn. It is home to a large selection of silver and gold jewellery, which is hand crafted by Katie Denby. Katie also does commissions and repair work. There are also wooden gifts, pottery and minerals for sale. An upstairs gallery features a permanent exhibition of oil and watercolour paintings by Dales artists – including Joanna Denby. Dotted around the shop you will also find many antiques and curiosities.

Opening Times 10.30am to 5.30pm seven days a week.

Address 51a Main Street, Grassington

Contact 01756 752605 • www.grassington.co.uk

6 *Bolton Abbey*

Bolton Abbey Iron-Art

I first saw the work of Bolton Abbey Iron-Art at a craft fair at Harewood House and was impressed enough to pick up a card.

If you want to see beautiful individually-crafted steel garden and dining-room furniture, and also enjoy a drive through wonderful countryside, you should visit here.

Bolton Abbey Iron-Art also makes gates, railings, wrought iron work, and provides a renovation service.

Opening Times It is advisable to telephone before visiting.

Address Newholme, Harrogate Road, Beamsley

Contact 01756 710268

7 *Embsay*

Embsay Needlecraft Centre

The fact that people travel from as far as Scotland and Norfolk on a day trip to visit the Embsay Needlecraft Centre is testimony to this shop's great appeal. It's no wonder when you see what the centre has to offer.

Embsay Mills Needlecraft Centre is in part of an old mill in the village of Embsay and has become a firm favourite with needle-workers throughout the country. Its specialist shop has different areas to cater for the many different needs of needleworkers.

There are all the top brands of threads, yarns and kits together with all kinds of craft fabrics. A large selection of print and tramme canvasses are on show, together with a wide choice of needlecraft furniture, daylight and magnifying lamps, needlecraft accessories, workboxes and equipment. You can browse through the shelves and racks in a separate room for books and publications.

The patchwork and quilting department carries a wonderful range of products, including fabrics, cushion panels, wadding, frames, rubber stamps, templates and patchwork and quilting accessories.

If you are just along for the ride and not needlework crazy then there is a coffee shop here where you can wait until the shopping expedition is over.

The centre also offers a range of courses and workshops throughout the year that cover a wide range of crafts and are run by qualified and experienced tutors. These cater for the beginner as well as the more advanced needlecrafter.

Opening Times The mill is opposite the well-known Embsay Steam Railway and is open seven days a week from 10am to 5pm.

Address Embsay Mills, Embsay

Contact 01756 700946

8 *Skipton*

Avena Herbal Products

If you are seeking a feeling of well-being (aren't we all) then pop into Avena Herbal Products. This family business specialises in creating pure natural products such as aromatherapy ointments and massage oils and handmade soaps.

Opening Times 9am to 5pm Monday, Wednesday, Thursday and Friday, 9am to 5.30pm Saturday, 11am to 5pm Tuesday.

Address The Kiosk, 8 Victoria Square, Skipton

Contact 01756 701636/792768

Stanforths Pork Pie Establishment

People queue impatiently outside the Skipton premises of Stanforths Pork Pie Establishment, their mouths watering as the smell of pork pies with hot runny jelly cooking inside wafts out of the door to greet them. As soon as they make their purchase they more often than not stand outside the shop and eat it, with jelly running down their chins! Such is the appeal and reputation of Stanforths pork pies.

The business was established in about 1925 and, as well as pork pies, this well-known butcher's deals in home-cured bacon and its own sausages. Mainly a pork butcher's, making black puddings, savoury ducks and the like, it also sells beef and lamb.

It is known more than anything, however, for its glorious pork pies, which are made and baked on the premises. These are all individually made and the same recipe has been used since they were first made.

Stanforths customers have taken its pie all over the world to former Skipton folk who dream of the pies while living abroad. These have sometimes been confiscated at customs!

Opening Times 6am to 5pm Monday, Wednesday, Thursday and

Friday. 6am to 1pm Tuesday. 6am to 4pm Saturday. Closed Sunday.
Address 9-11 Mill Bridge, Skipton
Contact 01756 793477

Whitakers

From small beginnings in 1889, the Whitaker family is a prime example of what is possible with hard work and a commitment to high standards and top quality products. For what started as a grocer's shop in the village of Crosshills well over a century ago has now grown into a business of worldwide renown.

The story of Whitakers Chocolatiers (Skipton) Limited is an inspiring one. The Crosshills grocery shop was started by husband and wife John and Rebecca Whitaker, and staffed with the help of their children Reg and Ida. Ida trained as a baker at Morecambe and on her return persuaded her father to change his grocer's shop into a baker's and confectioner's. Ida began making chocolates in 1903, taught by the wife of the vicar of Kildwick.

In 1926 the shop was transferred to its present site at Skipton High Street, and a restaurant was opened above it. In 1934 Reg married Claire Smith, an employee of the company. The couple went on to have four children – John, Fred, Peter and Susan.

In 1940 the restaurant was closed and Ida decided to leave the firm. She died in 1957. After the war the family decided to re-enter the restaurant business and leased the premises above the shop to other operators, and it has remained this way to the present day.

After Reg's death Claire spent most of the rest of her life running the family shop in the High Street as well as overseeing the development of chocolate manufacture on the site of the old bakery in Skipton, forming Whitakers Chocolatiers (Skipton) Limited in 1961.

Young John entered the business in 1955 and helped develop the chocolate side. Gradually this began to expand through sales to pubs, hotels, restaurants and shops.

In 1964 the family decided to expand the business and set about developing the chocolate side further. One of the chocolates selected was a mint flavoured product derived from an old nougatine recipe used by Claire's sister, Mrs Margery Smales, who had worked for the company previously. Eventually this product became an international winner and is currently exported to more than 25 countries as well as being served with coffee in thousands of outlets in the UK.

In 1988, foil wrapped products were introduced and now more than 50 per cent of Whitakers products are foiled, primarily crèmes, crisps and truffles – a large proportion of which are sold abroad. The distinctive Whitakers foil design consists of a candlelabra with three lighted candles, an idea inspired from the piano of Liberace, and the three candlelabra form the letter W.

Whitakers High Street shop was refurbished in 1989 and renamed in honour of Claire. It now sells only chocolates and is overseen by John's daughter Sally.

Fourth generation chocolatier William, John's eldest son, is now the company's Managing Director. John is chairman.

The Whitakers story continues, with the company now a worldwide supplier of quality chocolates. It has now got its own distribution company and is developing new products all the time. An own label bar was being considered at the time of writing.

Opening Times The Whitakers High Street shop is open 9am to 5pm Monday to Saturday, 10am to 4pm Sunday.

Address 85 Keighley Road, Skipton • **Contact** 01756 792531

Address Whitakers Shop, High Street, Skipton
Contact 01756 700240

9 *Cowling*

Brent Gallery

I remember meeting the very agreeable David Binns on a number of occasions when I worked as a reporter at the *Craven Herald*, usually to report his latest great artistic creation. Having done a fair amount of painting myself I am always amazed at the detail in David's work and admire his considerable talent.

David is one of this country's best known wildlife artists and is a member of the prestigious Society of Wildlife Artists, regularly exhibiting at the annual exhibition in The Mall, London. At these exhibitions he has won the RSPB Fine Art Award an unprecedented four times – in 1990, 1992, 1993 and 1994.

The Brent Gallery is run by David's wife Molly and features a wonderful display of his original watercolours and prints. His work is also on show at The Dalesmade Centre at Watershed Mill, Settle.

David is the son of artist and teacher Dan Binns and was born in Sutton-in-Craven and educated at Skipton and Leeds. His teaching career eventually took him back to his old school, Ermysted's Grammar School at Skipton, as head of the art department. He then spent a dozen years as a freelance artist living in Northumberland, overlooking the famous Lindisfarne nature reserve, which further fuelled his fondness for seabirds and, in particular, eiders.

David's work is very distinctive and its dexterity has led to a considerable amount of commercial work, including illustration, jigsaw designs for John Waddington, RSPB and RSNC, and cards for Medici Society and Rustcraft.

The Brent Gallery at Cowling opened in 1987 and stages regular exhibitions as well as permanent displays of works. You will also find etchings and wood engravings, ceramics, pottery, and jewellery and cards on sale here.

Opening Times 10.30am to 12 noon and 2pm to 5pm each day. Closed all day Wednesday and Saturday afternoons.

Address David Binns Fine Art, 60A Keighley Road, Cowling

Contact 01535 636892

10 *Kildwick*

Spinning Jenny

Discerning stitchers everywhere will find much to delight them and to help them create stitching masterpieces at Spinning Jenny at The Old Smithy at Kildwick.

A needlework specialist shop, Spinning Jenny is a treasure trove of all that is newest and best in embroidery and any enthusiast will spend hours in here spoilt for choice – relative novices such as myself will find much to inspire them. All the top needlework names are here and a superb range of quality cross-stitch kits is in stock, together with charts and books explaining the various needlework techniques and cross-stitch designs.

A large tapestry section features a range of stock and there is also furniture sold for you to apply your finished tapestries to. This includes stools, tables, workboxes and firescreens.

If you like to design your own work, Spinning Jenny carries a huge selection of evenweave fabrics in cotton and linen. There is also a selection of ready-made tablecloths and cushions, printed for you to embroider, and towels and bibs with ribbon-band for you to personalise.

From the small amount of stitching I have done (I started a tapestry about three years ago and keep meaning to finish it), I recognise only too well the need for magnification. Spinning Jenny can help here, with a range of products that includes magnifying lamps and spectacles and round-the-neck magnifiers.

You will have a field day in this shop, whether you are an experienced stitcher or a complete beginner. If you simply have an appreciation of this fine craft you can always buy some of the completed work that is on sale. There is also a display of worked models that changes regularly.

If you are looking for gift ideas for a needleworker relative or friend then Spinning Jenny is well worth a visit. For here you will find much inspiration, with gifts such as needle holders, enamelled scissor pendants and jewellery to choose from.

Opening Times 10am to 5pm Monday to Friday, 2pm to 5pm
Saturday. Closed Sundays, Bank Holidays, Easter weekend and
Christmas to New Year.
Address The Old Smithy, Kildwick
Contact 01535 632469

 *Ilkley*

Humphreys

Exclusive confectionery, which you can watch being made while
savouring the glorious aroma, is available from Humphreys at
Ilkley.

This family-run shop specialises in handmade chocolate and David
Humphreys is a master of the craft after his continental training
and long experience in the art of chocolate making. His research of
all the very best chocolate recipes has helped him develop a superb
range. How about Swiss style truffles filled with champagne or
some old fashioned rose and violet creams to get your taste buds
going?

In addition to a scrumptious range of filled chocolates, there is a
selection of novelty products. These include chocolate chess sets
and teddy bears.

Opening Times 9am to 5pm Monday to Saturday from October to
April. 9.30am to 5pm Wednesday, Thursday, Friday, and 9am to
5pm Saturday the rest of the year.
Address 16 Leeds Road, Ilkley
Contact 01943 609477 • www.exclusive-chocolates.co.uk

David Lishman Butchers

The old adage 'they don't make 'em like they used to' was obviously
initiated by someone who had never tasted the sausages of David
Lishman Butchers at Ilkley. Here they make sausages far better!

I was at the award-winning General Tarleton at Ferrensby a couple of weeks ago and saw David Lishman's champion sausages being given special mention on the menu board. The General Tarleton is sister to the Angel at Hetton and serves an equally superb range of culinary delights. That it chooses to promote David Lishman's products is testimony to their true quality.

Many other top local establishments also call on David Lishman for their sausages, which have officially been voted the best in Britain. For sausages are increasingly becoming more and more trendy, both in the home and in upmarket restaurants the length and breadth of the country, and Lishman's traditional, champion British rare breed pork sausages are going down a storm.

Over the years, David has been extremely proud to win many prestigious awards for his pork sausages, which come from his own Saddleback, Tamworth and Gloucester Old Spot rare breed pigs that are farm-reared at nearby Darley. Fed on a natural grain diet and allowed to grow at their own pace, which is reflected in the quality and taste of the end product, the three breeds are endangered species. If there was not a demand for their produce they could well disappear altogether.

David creates such sausage delicacies as guinea fowl and ginger, pork and black pudding, pork with Boddingtons beer, and pork, orange and mango. Mmmmmm!

His success has seen the size of his Ilkley shop grow considerably since he first started up in business in the town in 1986. He gained valuable experience working for other well-known butchers after leaving school, before launching out on his own and taking over the long-established butcher's shop of Percy Driver and Son on the retirement of Percy's son Edward. This is now a wonderful butcher's shop and people are often to be seen queuing out of the door, waiting to buy sausages, dry-cured rare breed back bacon, or some of the other goodies available here – and well worth the queue.

David's many titles include Yorkshire champion sausage maker and national Supreme Champion of Champions. He is also a leading member of the Guild of Q Butchers, a national organisation promoting quality throughout the industry. David joined a group of fellow Guild members in posing for the Guild's Charity Millennium Calendar (following the lead of the WI ladies from Rylstone), although not entirely in their birthday suits. Apparently, David is located middle back showing off his bacon!

Opening Times 7.30am to 5.30pm Monday to Friday, 7.30am to 4.30pm Saturday. Closed Sunday.

Address Leeds Road, Ilkley

Contact 01943 609436 • www.lishmans.co.uk

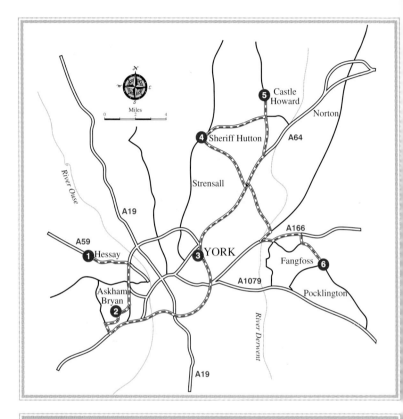

1 Hessay
Get Ahead Hats

2 Askham Bryan
Ainsty Farms Direct

3 York
Cox of Yorkshire
Droopy and Browns
Heraldic Art and Design
Mulberry Hall
Pyramid Gallery
Ken Spelman

4 Sheriff Hutton
York Wines

5 Castle Howard
Jorvik Glass

6 Fangfoss
Fangfoss Pottery
Harry Posthill
The Rocking Horse Shop

York

Introduction

For city centre shopping York is my favourite destination. Its combination of high street and independent shops set within historic city walls and along cobbled streets is difficult to beat.

There is something magical about this city, where Roman, Viking and medieval history combines. From its walls and gateways to the majestic York Minster, this is a place you will want to visit time and time again. There are a number of fine medieval churches, several excellent museums, including the National Railway Museum, and the ever-popular Jorvik Viking Centre in Coppergate.

Shopping here is an adventure. You can explore either the modern shopping area or visit The Shambles – narrow, cobbled streets with fine shops and cafés. Street names are somewhat strange and look out for the narrow passageways between them known as snickelways.

Shopping areas you should visit include Stonegate, where you will find Mulberry Hall, one of the world's leading fine china and crystal specialists with no less than 17 showrooms, and Droopy and Brown's, an old-fashioned shop selling its own range of striking women's clothes and accessories. Little Bettys Café is also nearby.

There are also rare books to be found, hand-produced embroideries at Heraldic Art and Design (York), and much, much more.

Drive a short distance out of York and you will discover The Rocking Horse Shop at Fangfoss, where talented craftsman Anthony Dew and his team create the most beautiful hand-carved rocking horses. In Fangfoss remember to call and see pine furniture maker Harry Postill, and to visit Fangfoss Pottery at The Old School.

If real-life horses are more your thing and you are off to the races, make sure you give Get Ahead Hats at Dutton Farm near Hessay a call first where you can hire a hat or have one specially made.

Hessay

Get Ahead Hats

I think hats epitomise sophistication and put me in mind of screen icons such as Audrey Hepburn and her timeless elegance. Today, however, they are both under-worn and generally overpriced – a state of affairs Beryl Otley from Dutton Farm near Hessay is fast changing with her successful franchise business Get Ahead Hats.

After struggling to find a hat for her daughter's wedding some years ago, and finding herself with more time on her hands, Beryl

decided to train in the craft of millinery and set up in business as Get Ahead Hats. She hasn't looked back since – although plenty of other people have at her hats. There are now 14 Get Ahead Hats franchises throughout the country – four here in Yorkshire, and all based at either farms or country houses.

Get Ahead Hats designs, makes and hires and sells a stunning range of headwear for all those important occasions in your life. Ascot would be honoured to have any one of the Get Ahead Hats' creations grace its big day and Beryl's ethos that special hats don't have to mean a 'special' price will leave you with money to place a few bets if you wish.

At Get Ahead Hats you can either hire or buy an item from the shop, which will be fitted for you, or have a couture hat hand-made to order. It will be made exactly to your requirements and wishes. If you want a hat retrimming then Beryl and her team will do that for you too.

Beryl's business has grown considerably since she started and she now employs a London-trained designer and two other trained milliners. They are kept extremely busy and new franchises are opening all the time, with all the new franchisees being taught the craft of millinery.

It is a very friendly team and you are always assured a warm welcome when you visit a Get Ahead Hats shop. In Yorkshire these are at Park Farm House, Main Road, Burton Agnes; Staindale Grange Farm, near Hornby, Great Smeaton, Northallerton, and Ranelands Farm, Hebden, near Skipton.

Opening Times "Flexible" says Beryl, and evening appointments are available.

Address Dutton Farm, Near Hessay, York

Contact 01904 738656 • www.getaheadhats.co.uk

 ② *Askham Bryan*

Ainsty Farms Direct

Six farmers in the York area have joined together to form Ainsty Farms Direct and according to Beryl Otley, of Get Ahead Hats at Dutton Farm, they do the best beefburgers going.

The members of Ainsty Farms Direct – Phillip Hughes, Jeremy Gill, Sam Blacker, Peter Pick, John Barnes and Stuart Beaton – share a commitment to producing quality full flavour meat, a genuine concern for the environment and a free-range approach to rearing their livestock.

They produce and sell direct to individuals prime beef, fresh lamb and succulent pork. You can also find this for sale at farmers' markets in the York area.

Address 118 Main Street, Askham Bryan, York

Contact 01904 705437

③ *York*

Cox of Yorkshire

Cox of Yorkshire, home to a range of leather and sheepskin products, was established in 1921 and is said to be York's original sheepskin shop. Prior to this it was a butcher's and as late as 1938 pigs and sheep used to be driven down a passageway to a slaughterhouse at the side of the shop,

Traditional shoe and leather goods repairs are carried out on the premises, a craft that has been passed down through the generations over the last three quarters of a century.

Opening Times 9am to 5.30pm Monday to Saturday, 11am to 4pm Sunday.

Address 30/32 The Shambles, York

Contact 01904 624449 • www.coxofyorkshire.co.uk

Droopy and Browns

You may well think that Droopy and Browns is an odd name for a shop, but the name is distinctive – just like the wonderful range of women's clothes Droopy and Browns designs, manufactures and sells.

Apparently the name was arrived at the day before the first Droopy and Browns shop was due to open in

York back in 1972 and the partners were still unsure what to call it. All the suggested names evoked a trendy boutique image that was not conducive to the clothes and shopping ambience they wanted to create. It was remarked that the shop was not like that at all – that it was sort of droopy and brown. And the name stuck.

The shop's old-fashioned style and emphasis on quality cut clothes and a level of service that reflects a bygone age make this shop a real treat. The company has gone on to open other branches, but its headquarters remain firmly ensconced in York.

Opening Times 9.30am to 5.30pm Monday to Friday, 9.30am to 6pm Saturday. Closed Sunday.

Address Stonegate, York

Contact 01904 621458

Heraldic Art and Design (York)

The Heraldic Art and Design (York) shop in The Shambles specialises in coats of arms that are hand-embroidered in gold and silver threads. It also does regimental and club insignia, logos, banners and blazer patches, and produces hand-painted arms and calligraphy showing the origins of a name. It can trace and produce a coat of arms for most names of European origin.

Embroideries are by far the most popular item. An average embroidery takes about 50 hours to produce and is made using 22-carat gold and sterling silver threads and French silks. The most requested embroidery is a 'wedding double', a coat of arms for his and her family names mounted side by side and with a parchment label on the mount underneath that shows in calligraphy the couple's names and the date and place of the wedding. This is also very popular as an anniversary gift.

As everything is made by hand it is all made to order and the average delivery time is 10 weeks.

Opening Times The shop is normally open every day from 10.30am (11am on Sundays).

Address 43 The Shambles, York

Contact 01904 672906 • www.heraldic-art.co.uk

Mulberry Hall

There can be few places where you will find a display of china and crystal as fine as the one at Mulberry Hall in Stonegate, York. It is vast and includes all the very best names, including Halcyon Days, Herend, Meissen, Wedgwood, Royal Copenhagen, Baccarat, Royal Crown Derby, Lladro, and many, many more.

Mulberry Hall is one of the world's leading fine china and crystal specialists and while here you may like to visit its café for some refreshment.

The building itself dates from 1434. There is also a dining warehouse, where you will find all the best designer names for the kitchen, such as Magimix, Villeroy and Boch.

Opening Times 9am to 5.30pm Monday to Saturday. Closed Sunday.

Address Stonegate, York

Contact 01904 620736 • www.mulberryhall.co.uk

Pyramid Gallery

In a 15th century building owned by the National Trust in Stonegate you will find the Pyramid Gallery and all the contemporary arts and crafts it has to offer, including the work of around 50 designer jewellers.

This is a lovely gallery to browse round and it houses a first-class selection of British-made contemporary crafts, jewellery and original prints. There is the work of many leading designers on show, including glass, ceramics, wood and metal, as well as jewellery.

Two upstairs galleries have regularly changing exhibitions and are always worth a look.

Opening Times 10am to 5pm Monday to Friday, 10am to 5.30pm Saturday, and 11am to 4.30pm Sunday.

Address 43 Stonegate, York

Contact 01904 641187

Ken Spelman

Book shops always hold a very special appeal to me – I am in awe of all those shelves of books, each one containing a wonderful world of its own. If you share this love of bookshops you should pay a visit to Ken Spelman at 70 Micklegate, York – home to over 40,000 rare and out of print books.

Ken Spelman was established in York in 1948, although the site had been a bookshop since the beginning of the century. It now occupies all four floors of this Micklegate building and also features a gallery area displaying early English watercolours.

Opening Times 9am to 5.30pm Monday to Saturday.

Address 70 Micklegate, York

Contact 01904 624414 • www.kenspelman.com

④ *Sheriff Hutton*

York Wines

Fine wine is one of life's necessities, in my opinion that is, and so finding this little shop in the village of Sheriff Hutton was a nice surprise.

York Wines – Specialist Wine Importers was established 15 years ago by Stuart Vass at his home in York, as an extension of a hobby. He was working as catering manager at a local college at the time. The business grew and he moved to Sheriff Hutton and opened a small specialist wine shop, which also stocks a range of local beers.

All the wines sold at York Wines are exclusive to the shop in this area and you can get a bottle of wine from £1.99 to £175.

Opening Times Monday to Tuesday 10am to 5pm, Wednesday to Saturday 10am to 8pm.

Address Wellington House, Sheriff Hutton, York

Contact 01347 878546 • www.yorkwines.co.uk

⑤ *Castle Howard*

Jorvik Glass

Set in the grounds of Castle Howard you will find Jorvik Glass, which was established by Angela Henderson in 1995.

During a visit here you can watch the traditional techniques of this craft at close quarters in the hot glass studio and see some of the exquisite items made. A wide range of glassware, both functional and decorative, is made on the premises. This includes perfume bottles, paperweights, jewellery, animals, wine glasses and decanters, vases and bowls.

Opening Times 10am to 5pm seven days a week between March and December.

Address Castle Howard, The Stable Yard, York

Contact 01653 648555

Fangfoss

Fangfoss Pottery

The Fangfoss Pottery has been going since 1977, when it was started by Gerry and Lyn Grant, and is now a well-established business. In addition to making commemorative items, the pottery also produces a wide range of domestic ware and gift items that can be viewed in the upstairs showroom.

Opening Times 9am to 5pm Monday to Friday. Also open most weekends. Telephone first to avoid disappointment.

Address The Old School, Fangfoss

Contact 01759 368384

Harry Postill

Harry Postill pine furniture maker could always be excused for going to sleep on the job, for the bulk of his creations are beds! Harry's Wooden Beds feature a wide range of styles and woods, all created at his sawdust-filled workshop at The Old Chapel, Fangfoss. Just along the road one way is his showroom; just along the road the other way is his house.

It was always Harry's ambition to have a house with workshop and showroom in the countryside and now he is a happy man. The workshop is in an old Primitive Methodist Chapel that dates back to 1865, although there used to be a joiner's shop on the site before that.

Harry is well known for his beds, but also makes a range of other items that includes tables, wardrobes and dressers.

Opening Times 8am to 5.30pm Monday to Friday, 9.30am to 4.30pm Saturday. Closed Sundays.

Address The Old Chapel, Fangfoss, York

Contact 01759 368209

The Rocking Horse Shop

When I was a young girl I remember having great fun playing on a rocking horse made by my grandfather – a toy far removed from some of the garish, noisy and badly-made excuses for play things my two daughters now both have and crave. I think, like me, people now hanker for some good old-fashioned quality and you will see plenty of this when you visit The Rocking Horse Shop at Fangfoss.

Its superb range of fine wooden rocking horses evokes memories of an era when play was simple and straightforward – and enormous fun. Having said that, apparently they were not toys originally but rather devices designed to help children ride.

The man behind this highly successful venture is Anthony Dew, who has written books on the craft and formed The Guild of Rocking Horse Makers, a unique worldwide association. He has also launched the successful quarterly publication The Rocking Horse and Toy magazine.

Anthony has over 20 years experience of his craft and has used it to create a dazzling range of rocking horses. These include beautiful hand carved creatures on stands or bow rockers, which you can commission in any size and colour. Anthony has also created an extensive selection of rocking horse designs that you can use yourself to make your very own rocking horse. My daughters were given one of Anthony's Toddlers Rocking Horse designs for Christmas some years ago and it really is brilliant. No matter how hard they rocked they never fell off.

In addition to the popular designs and rocking horse kits that you can buy here, or via mail order, The Rocking Horse Shop also supplies an exhaustive range of accessories and fittings for both rocking horse makers and restorers. So whether you want glass eyes, real or simulated horsehair mane and tail, leather bridle and reins, you can get it all here. Also available are tools and equipment.

You will thoroughly enjoy your visit here because not only is there a large shop to look round, where you can see The Rocking Horse Shop's dolls house and sports car designs alongside the newly-finished rocking horses, there is also a museum of old rocking horses. This is a unique collection of fascinating creations, which Anthony has collected over the years.

All the new rocking horses are created on site and they are exclusive to this shop. The Rocking Horse Shop also provides a full restoration service.

Anthony is a master of his craft and a great source of information on rocking horses. Apparently slab or board sided rocking horses appeared in the early part of the 17th century. The fully carved horses mounted on thin arcs of timber came in the 18th century, and this bow rocker style of horse became known and loved as the archetypal rocking horse. In the 1880s the swing iron safety stand was developed and this remains in widespread use today.

Mass production methods saw large-scale wooden rocking horse manufacture decline during the early 20th century, but thankfully people like Anthony and cottage industries like The Rocking Horse Shop are keeping the craft well and truly alive. A shopping trail must.

Opening Times 9am to 4pm Monday to Saturday.

Address Fangfoss, York

Contact 01759 368737 • www.rockinghorse.co.uk

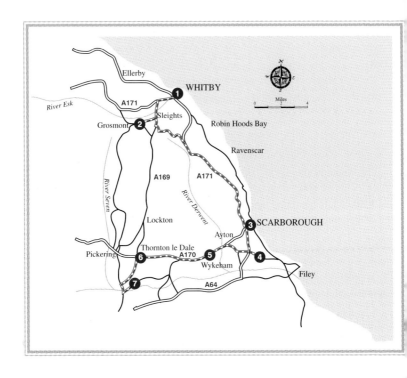

1 Whitby
Bobbins
Elizabeth Botham And Sons Ltd
Eagle Turnery
The Enamel Workshop
Harbourside Pottery
The Studio of John Freeman
Michael Pybus Fine Arts
The Sutcliffe Gallery
Wash House Pottery

2 Grosmont
The Grosmont Gallery

3 Scarborough
Books and Bygones

4 Killerby
The Stained Glass Centre

5 Wykeham
Ankaret Cresswell

6 Thornton le Dale
Thornton-le-Dale Arts and Crafts

7 High Marishes
Sophie Hamilton Pottery

The Coast

Introduction

Oh we do like to be beside the seaside, and in Yorkshire that takes us to the popular resort of Scarborough and picturesque smaller destinations such as Filey, Whitby, Robin Hood's Bay and Staithes.

All have their own special appeal. Take the appealing fishing port of Whitby where time, as they say, seems to have stood still with little changed over the years. Whitby Abbey perched up on the clifftop (and which inspired the writing of Bram Stoker's *Dracula*), and the Whitby Jet and Enamel Workshop in Church Street, are just two of the places visitors always flock to. Another is Whitby Museum, where you can discover the story of the town's most famous inhabitant, Captain James Cook.

Whitby and its harbour, together with the town's narrow alleys and quaint streets will win you over in an instant with their timeless charm and unique character. The historic 'East Side' of Whitby is my favourite for shopping, with its old buildings, cobbles, and wide range of shops. It is this part of Whitby that is home to a shop that will send any knitter into a frenzy and get their needles clicking. For Bobbins is a rare find, where husband and wife team Dick and Pam Hoyle have created what has been referred to as a 'knitter's paradise'.

Scarborough is a bustling place attracting visitors back year after year with its beaches and seaside entertainments. Here you will see Scarborough Castle and there is also the Sealife Centre to explore.

Among the many seaside-type shops selling sunhats and sun lotion (who must incidentally rely on two months' takings to carry them through the rest of Britain's year), there are many individual shops you may like to pop into for a browse.

This is a popular area with artists and you will stumble across many galleries and potteries, often being able to see the residents at work.

 *Whitby*

Bobbins

If you are a knitter you may well think you have died and gone to heaven when you visit Bobbins, a wool, crafts and antiques shop located in the red brick Wesley Hall off the cobbles of Church Street.

The Hall was previously a Church School and dates back to 1901 and forms an intriguing backdrop to the displays inside.

Opened in 1983 by Dick and Pam Hoyle, Bobbins stocks a wide range of wools. These include Colinette hand-painted yarns, Rowan yarns, 5-ply Guernsey wool, denim cotton, and their own Arans.

Over the years the emphasis of their business has changed, with a great demand today for made-up garments. They employ a band of home knitters who make a range of fabulous traditional-style garments.

Bobbins also has its own exclusive range of Knit-Kits. These include kits for traditional fishermen's ganseys. A gansey is a hardwearing wool sweater worn by fishermen around the coast of Britain for many years. The gansey developed into a tradition with a variety of fascinating local and family patterns. Apparently, fishermen wore their gansies all the time and had a 'Sunday best' one for church, and young women often knitted their intended husbands a 'wedding shirt' gansey to get married in.

Bobbins has created its own range of gansey patterns, each from a different town or village on the East Coast of Yorkshire. It also offers an impressive range of other exclusive knitwear designs.

Look out for the aspiring model in the Bobbins' literature sporting a distinctive fisherman look with his wonderful full beard and moustache – its none other than Dick Hoyle.

The couple have been in business since 1977, starting off at Robin Hood's Bay, and later opening a shop at York. Now they are firmly ensconced at Whitby with a far-reaching reputation as one of the country's best wool shops.

They will mail yarns anywhere in the world and if they don't have something in stock they will do their very best to get it for you.

Opening Times Bobbins is open seven days a week, all year round, from 10am until about 5pm.

Address Wesley Hall, Church Street, Whitby

Contact 01947 600585 • www.bobbins.co.uk

Elizabeth Botham and Sons Limited

Elizabeth Botham and Sons Limited is something of a Whitby tradition, having been a family-run craft bakery in the fishing port since 1865.

Using its own original recipes, the company creates such baking wonders as Botham's Yorkshire Brack, Original Whitby Gingerbread, Plum Bread, and also its own range of handmade preserves and chutneys. Just being launched at the time of writing is a new line of Sticky Stem Ginger Brack featuring a winning combination of the finest stem ginger, golden sultanas and orange zest. Botham's also has its own special blend of tea and a unique coffee.

Appropriately, as the creator of so much delicious home-baked fare and fine drink, Elizabeth Botham and Sons Limited has shops, a café and restaurant in the town which needless to say prove very popular.

At Skinner Street there is a shop and restaurant, and at Baxtergate a shop and café. Testimony to the company's high standards is the fact that the restaurant has just been awarded Membership of The Guild of Tea Shops by the Tea Council.

Although Elizabeth Botham and Sons Limited retains much of its original traditional charm it is a very forward-thinking company and has been at the forefront of the use of modern technology to further the success of its business. It carried off a major award at the Yorkshire Website Awards 2000 for its excellent website that has allowed this small bakery to market its products worldwide.

Opening Times Shops open 8.30am to 5.15pm Monday to Saturday, closing at 4.45pm on Wednesday. Restaurant and Café open 9.30am to 5pm.

Address 35/39 Skinner Street, Whitby

Contact 01947 602823 • www.botham.co.uk

Eagle Turnery

At the Eagle Turnery in Whitby's Hunter Street you will find items created from wood that show off its natural beauty and fabulous graining.

Woodturner Nik Harty works on the premises making a unique range of products, including bowls, wall and mantle clocks, vases, candlesticks, earring stands and boxes.

Nik specialises in reclaiming wood that has been either used or discarded as unusable and transforms it into something stunning. Often he uses any fault with the wood as the focal point of the finished piece.

During a visit you can not only see his wonderful creations, you can also watch Nik at work.

Opening Times 9am to 6pm most days. It is advisable to telephone first if you are travelling a long way. When the lathe is running Nik does not hear the phone – so keep trying!

Address The Dell, 8 Hunter Street, Whitby

Contact 01947 821205 • www.eagleturnery.fsnet.co.uk

The Enamel Workshop

Whitby is famous for the beautiful ancient black gemstone jet that has been found here and crafted into stunning jewellery by a band of local craftspeople for many, many years.

Today The Enamel Workshop is one of several shops in Whitby selling jewellery handmade on these premises and featuring Whitby jet.

You will find The Enamel Workshop close to the Abbey steps in the historic old town. Formerly a fisherman's cottage and bakehouse, its large oak-beamed fireplace is filled with displays of Whitby jet, original handmade silver jewellery, and an extensive range of amber jewellery.

Whitby is very popular with the Gothic movement. Thousands of people visit every year for Gothic weekends – probably something to do with its connection with Bram Stoker's story *Dracula* – and a range of Gothic Whitby jet jewellery is now available here.

It is thought that jet mining took place in the Whitby area in the Bronze Age, but its boom years were in the Victorian era. Around 1,500 people were employed in the industry at the port's manufacturing shops.

Men known as 'jetties' used to make a living out of supplying jet and fossils to local craftsmen. The jet was obtained from cliffs, or by mining in caves.

There is evidence of jet jewellery far back into history. Burial places of bronze-age people who lived 10,000 years ago have often been found to contain jet beads. It is said that the shiny black stone was worn to ward off evil spirits (perhaps I will start wearing that jet bracelet my parents gave me years ago!).

The Romans also had a great liking for jet, and Chaucer talks of a Gate of bright black stone found in Yorkshire and worn by followers of fashion in the 14th century.

It seems that around the years of 1840 to 1860 jet jewellery started to be bought by families of people who had died and eventually this marked a decline in its popularity. Today jet is a much-loved gemstone once again, with people drawn to its unique qualities.

A wide range of jet jewellery is available and a visit to The Enamel Workshop will reveal some fine examples.

Opening Times The Enamel Workshop is open 10am to 5pm seven days a week from Easter to October 31, and most weekends throughout the year.

Address 128 Church Street, Whitby

Contact 01947 606216

Harbourside Pottery

Former teacher Terry Shone whiles away his hours happily creating pots at the Harbourside Pottery, which can be found down a little alley in Grape Lane.

There is no shortage of demand for Terry's work and he sometimes struggles to make enough pots to keep up with requests.

His eye-catching slipware pottery includes a range for domestic use, such as bowls, tapas dishes and mugs, one-off exhibition pieces and commemorative ware.

You can see him at work in his workshop when you visit the shop.

Opening Times 11am until 4pm most days.

Address 19 Grape Lane, Whitby

Contact 01947 603029

The Studio of John Freeman

An artist of some repute, John Freeman established his studio in Whitby in 1969 and is now well known for his studies of Whitby and the surrounding area. You can now find him working at a studio in a converted slaughterhouse and butcher's shop in the heart of Whitby's historic 'East Side'.

Opening Times 9.30am to 5pm, Monday to Saturday, and 10.30am to 5pm on Sunday.

Address 9 Market Place, Whitby

Contact 01947 602799 • www.johnfreemanstudio.co.uk

Michael Pybus Fine Arts

This is a shop where I could easily be tempted to spend some money, for it displays some superb artwork.

The studio and gallery of Michael Pybus is just below the 199 steps to the Abbey, and as well as Michael's own work in oil and watercolour there is the work of David Allen, David Curtis RSMA ROI, and William Dealtry on show.

Michael, who has exhibited in London and had a one-man exhibition at Scarborough Art Gallery, opened the gallery in 1998.

Opening Times 10.30am to 5pm seven days a week.

Address 127 Church Street, Whitby

Contact 01947 820028

The Sutcliffe Gallery

You will step back in time when you walk through the door of The Sutcliffe Gallery, for here is housed a fascinating collection of photographs taken by eminent Victorian photographer Frank Meadow Sutcliffe in and around Whitby between 1870 and 1910.

During the Victorian era Whitby was known as 'the photographer's mecca' due to the enormous visual appeal of its picturesque and character-filled scenes of fishing folk and harbour views. Frank Meadow Sutcliffe was one of the most famous of the photographers of this age.

He moved to Whitby with his family in 1870 and set up a tiny photography studio in a disused jet workshop in Waterloo Yard in 1875. He remained in the town and captured local life there in a stunning range of photographs with a strong artistic appeal.

Frank Meadow Sutcliffe was awarded over 60 medals at exhibitions around the globe and in this country between 1880 and 1894. In 1935 he was made an Honorary Fellow of the Royal Photographic Society.

Following his retirement from professional photography, he became the curator of Whitby Museum. He died in 1941, aged 88.

The wonderful sepia photographs at The Sutcliffe Gallery that capture priceless scenes from the past and feature weather-beaten faces and fishing folk are well worth a look.

Opening Times 9am to 5pm Monday to Saturday, 12 noon to 5pm Sunday.

Address 1 Flowergate, Whitby

Contact 01947 602239 • www.sutcliffe-gallery.co.uk

Wash House Pottery

You will find this quaint little pottery tucked away off the cobbled Church Street in the historic part of Whitby.

It is said to be Whitby's longest established working pottery and you can see a range of products being made in its tiny workshop. I particularly like the tiles, but there are also garden planters, house plaques and other items of pottery for sale.

Opening Times 10am to 5/5.30pm seven days a week.

Address 4 Blackburn's Yard, Whitby

Contact 01947 604995

 *Grosmont*

The Grosmont Gallery

Five miles from Whitby is Grosmont which attracts many people every year as it's the end of the North Yorkshire Steam Railway line. For me, however, there is another reason for visiting – and that's The Grosmont Gallery.

Set in an old wood mill, The Grosmont Gallery is one of those places where you want to stay awhile and enjoy both the ambience of the expansive gallery and the quality works on show.

This friendly gallery displays the work of around a dozen artists and eight potters, and also some very impressive iron work that is produced locally. Virtually all the pottery is made within six miles of Grosmont and the paintings the work of artists from within 30 miles.

The gallery belongs to Chris Geall and his family. Chris is a potter and painter and his stunning range of decorative and functional stoneware pottery is both made and sold at the gallery. His workshop is tucked away at the rear.

Chris, formerly a chemical engineer, only sells his work through the gallery and loves meeting visitors and chatting with them. He and his wife and three young children live above the gallery and consequently it is a very child-friendly place. There is even a children's play area to keep the little ones happy while mums and dads have a browse round.

The mill building was built at the end of the 19th century and has an interesting history, having been used as a funeral director's, garage, cinema, and as a gallery for 17 years by Anne and Paul Blackwell.

The gallery is situated right next to the end of the line of the North Yorkshire Steam Railway and is also home to a picture framing and restoration business.

Opening Times 10.30am until 5.30pm April – October.

Address Front Street, Grosmont, Whitby

Contact 01947 895007

 *Scarborough*

Books and Bygones

Must just give this little shop a quick mention. It draws the attention of almost every passer-by with its collection of old Dinky toys and tin toys in the window. I saw some Dinky toys exactly the same as some belonging to my dad that I used to play with as a child. You will also find old *Dandy* and *Beano* magazines here. A find worth sharing.

Address 20 Bar Street, Scarborough

❹ *Killerby*

Stained Glass Centre

There is something fascinating about stained glass windows. Perhaps it's their intricacy or the mesmerising effect of light transcending the vividly coloured glass.

A visit to the Stained Glass Centre at Killerby will fuel your fascination even further, for here you can witness stained glass being made and see an exhibition that charts the history of the craft and the processes involved in making a window.

The centre has an interesting history, which began back in 1884 when William Lazenby opened his stained glass works in Bradford. His sons and grandsons took up the craft and today his great granddaughter Valerie Green is carrying on the family tradition. She started the craft as a hobby and has not looked back since.

Valerie and her team both produce new stained glass and leaded lights and also carry out restoration and repair work.

Their services are much in demand, and His Royal Highness the

Duke of York has unveiled no less than three stained glass windows created at the Stained Glass Centre, and Her Majesty The Queen has unveiled another. A special commission for a window for the Northern Police Convalescent Home at Harrogate was one of those unveiled by HRH the Duke of York.

During a visit to the Stained Glass Centre you can also enjoy a visit to its showroom, which is full of stained glass lampshades, mirrors, candleholders, boxes, clocks, window hangings and gifts to buy.

You may like to rest a while and enjoy some home baking and light refreshments in The Tea Room, overlooking the garden and waterfall. If the weather allows you can take tea in the garden.

The Stained Glass Centre is situated just off the B1261 between the villages of Cayton and Lebberston. Visitors can watch stained glass being made on weekdays, but not at weekends or Bank Holidays.

Opening Times Daily from 10am until 5pm.

Address Killerby Lane, Killerby, near Cayton, Scarborough

Contact 01723 585465

www.yorkshire.co.uk/valgreen

 *Wykeham*

Ankaret Cresswell

Set in a wonderful building in the pretty village of Wykeham you can find real quality clothes at Ankaret Cresswell as well as a full size working handloom.

Since 1985 Ankaret Cresswell has been weaving woven wool fabrics and tailoring them into exclusive handmade suits and separates for both men and women. You will find absolutely nothing mass-produced about the clothes found here; rather a true sense of style and a superior level of fit.

If you are looking for quality made to measure clothing then Ankaret Cresswell is the place for you. A bespoke suit handmade from some of the exciting woven wool fabrics will have you feeling and looking a million dollars.

Ankaret Cresswell has also launched a range of furnishing fabrics.

Opening Times The shop is open Monday to Friday all year round, 9.30am until 4.30pm each day.

Address Wykeham, Scarborough

Contact 01723 864406 • www.ankaret-cresswell.co.uk

⑥ *Thornton le Dale*

Thornton-le-Dale Arts and Crafts

Here you will find work by local artists and craftspeople displayed in a stable block dating back to the 1700's.

Blue Robin Woodcrafts of Browside, Ravenscar, are one of the exhibitors, showing a range of hand-crafted wooden toys. Potter Sophie Hamilton from High Marishes also has her work on display.

Opening Times The gallery is open daily from 10am until 5pm.
Address Thornton-le-Dale
Contact 01751 477404

High Marishes

Sophie Hamilton

I could quite happily swap places with Sophie Hamilton for a
while. This talented young potter lives in her countryside home
with a nearby building converted into a pottery and surrounded by
fields. Cows can almost poke their heads through any open doors
and windows.

Here Sophie designs and creates her own distinctive range of
contemporary handmade pottery. A red, blue and gold sunflower
design has been a top seller for some time now.

A shop displays a full range of her work and people travel from
far and wide to visit.

Her attractive pottery is both functional and decorative with rich
coloured glazes and patterns. Recent commissions have included a
full dinner service.

You can also see Sophie's work displayed at her stall at Newgate
Market, York, every Saturday (just off Parliament Street, behind
the flower stall).

Opening Times The pottery is open 10am to 6pm Monday to
Friday, 2pm to 5pm Sunday (May to September). Closed between
Christmas and New Year.

Address The Pottery, High Marishes, Malton

Contact 01653 668228

www.touristnetuk.com/ne/sophie-hamilton

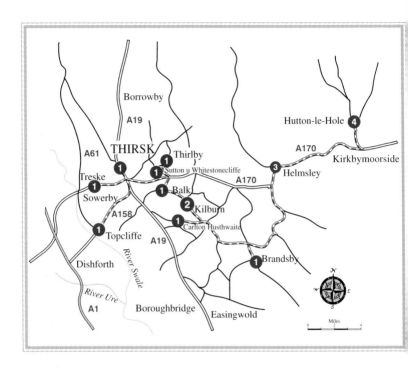

1 Thirsk Furniture Trail
Acorn Industries, *Bransby*
Colin Almack, *Sutton under Whitestonecliffe*
Design in Wood, *Thirsk*
English Hardwood Furniture, *Topcliffe*
Bob Hunter, *Thirlby*
Malcolm Pipes, *Carlton Husthwaite*
Old Mill Furniture, *Balk*
Treske Furniture, *Thirsk*

2 Kilburn
Robert Thompson's Craftsmen Ltd

3 Helmsley
The Bead Workshop
Dolly Mix
Hunters delicatessen
McLeods
The Stick Man

4 Hutton le Hole
Moorwax candles

The North York Moors

Introduction

The North York Moors National Park contains England's largest expanse of heather-covered moorland. Visit in late summer and you will find the heather in full bloom and forming a breathtaking purple carpet. There are also picturesque country towns offering traditional market days and historic houses for you to visit; and you will find no better walking territory, with dozens of scenic routes for you to enjoy.

The North York Moors is a honeypot for furniture makers, with the area around Thirsk home to more than half-a-dozen traditional craftsmen creating fine handmade furniture.

The Mouseman Visitor Centre at Kilburn is a must. Here you can learn more about the story of Robert Thompson, the village wheelwright, who became renowned as 'The Mouseman' furniture maker. A trademark mouse appears on all his oak furniture. I remember taking great delight as a child on 'The Mouseman' stand at the Great Yorkshire Show at Harrogate trying to find the mouse on all the pieces of furniture. Later, when proceedings dragged and mouse spotting was more fun than reporting a meeting of Skipton Town Council for the *Craven Herald*, I would do the same in the council chamber, which is furnished with Mouseman furniture.

You will find much to interest you at Helmsley, where in the picturesque setting of The Walled Garden Workshops you will find the beautiful hand-carved walking sticks of 'The Stick Man' Keith Pickering and be able to chat with him about his creations and see him at work.

While in the North York Moors area you can also visit one of the area's many stately homes and gardens, or take a trip on the steam railway that crosses the Moors from Grosmont to Pickering. There is a station at Goathland – the 'Aidensfield' of television's *Heartbeat* series.

① *Thirsk – Furniture Trail*

Old Mill Furniture

A 300-year-old restored former corn mill in the tiny hamlet of Balk, some three miles south-east of Thirsk, is home to Old Mill Furniture. Here you will find handmade furniture in solid hardwoods for every room in your house in both traditional and modern styles. Woods used include oak, walnut, maple, mahogany, cherry, elm, chestnut and ash.

The business is a partnership with Horace and Margaret Knight, and their sons Adrian and Jeremy. They work with a team of craftsmen to create a fabulous range of furniture. Each piece of furniture is handmade by an individual craftsman, from choosing the wood right through to final finishing.

There is a wide range of standard designs, and you can also have bespoke pieces made for your home or office.

Opening Times 9am to 5pm Monday to Saturday.

Address Balk, Thirsk

Contact 01845 597227 • www.theoldmill.co.uk

Treske Furniture

A member of the Thirsk Furniture Trail and a winner of a Green Apple award for environmental best practice, Treske Furniture produces modern furniture using English hardwoods handcrafted by its own trained cabinetmakers. It also has a Trees to Treske Visitor Centre (admission fee payable) which includes an award-winning exhibition about trees and furniture together with a tour of the factory and showrooms.

This small, friendly business was founded by the late John Gormley over a quarter of a century ago and is located in a beautiful old maltings building next to Thirsk station.

There is a gift shop with interesting wooden presents and pocket-money souvenirs and a tearoom serving drinks and home-made cakes and snacks. Outside there is a picnic area in the old orchard and a Millennium Maze playground. There are good views of trains on the main East Coast line from here!

Opening Times 10am to 5pm all year round. Closed Christmas week. The factory will not be working at weekends.

Address Station Works, Thirsk

Contact 01845 522770 • www.yorkshirenet.co.uk/treske

While in the Thirsk area don't miss calling in on other local craftsmen creating a range of stunning furniture, several easily distinguished by their unique trademark symbols such as a fox's mask and hand-carved wren. These include:

Acorn Industries

Bransby, York

Contact: 01347 888217

Opening Times: 8am to 5pm Monday to Friday, 9am to 1pm Saturday.

Colin Almack – Beaver Furniture

Beaver Lodge, Sutton under Whitestonecliffe, Thirsk

Telephone: 01845 597420

Opening Times: 8am to 5pm Monday to Friday, 8am to 4pm Saturday, 9am to 1pm Sunday.

Design in Wood

The Old Coach House, Chapel Street, Thirsk

Contact: 01845 525010 • www.designinwood.co.uk

Opening Times: 8.30am to 5pm Monday to Friday, or by appointment.

English Hardwood Furniture

The Mill Yard, Catton Lane, Topcliffe, Thirsk

Contact: 01845 578172

Opening Times: 10am to 5pm Monday to Saturday.

Bob Hunter – Wren Cabinet Makers

Pear Tree House, Thirlby, Thirsk

Contact: 01845 597453

Opening Times: 8am to 5pm Monday to Friday, 9am to 12 noon Saturday, other times by appointment.

Malcolm Pipes – Fox Furniture

The Old Hall Workshop, Carlton Husthwaite, Thirsk

Contact: 01845 501359 • www.brigantia.co.uk

Opening Times: 9am to 5pm Monday to Saturday and by appointment in the evening and on Sunday.

② *Kilburn*

Robert Thompson's Craftsmen Limited

Say 'The Mouseman' to most people and they instantly think of Robert Thompson's Craftsmen Limited, a distinctive range of unique hand-crafted English oak furniture bearing the trademark mouse symbol, and the man responsible for putting the pretty village of Kilburn on the world map.

Robert Thompson, who was born in 1876, gave his life to rekindling the craft of carving and joinery in English oak, and his name is now known throughout this country and the world for superbly crafted domestic and ecclesiastical furniture bearing the famous mouse symbol. It seems the history of this lovely little mouse character is somewhat unclear. Robert Thompson himself told the story that one of his craftsmen commented that they were all as poor as church mice and Robert proceeded to carve a mouse on the church rafter he was working on. This particular mouse has never been found, but the mouse has continued as the Robert Thompson's mark of quality ever since.

The work of Robert Thompson can be seen far and wide, including some splendid church furnishings, and today the craftsman's high standards and passion for his work are continued at Robert Thompson's Craftsmen Limited under the management of his grandsons and great grandsons. The company's headquarters are based in the Elizabethan timber framed cottage that was Robert Thompson's family home and now contains offices, showrooms and design department. In

the showroom you can see examples of fine Mouseman furniture. Special commissions are also undertaken.

When visiting the showroom you can also pop across the road to the Mouseman Visitor Centre and learn all about Robert Thompson and his work. Converted from the old joiner's and blacksmith's shop, the Visitor Centre gives you the chance to watch craftsmen at work carving in English oak. You will learn how Robert Thompson believed that the character of oak was lost if the timber had not been naturally seasoned. Consequently, large oak planks were stacked one on top of another, separated by wooden laths to allow air into each layer, for several years until they were prime for carving. This method is still used today at Kilburn.

The Mouseman Visitor Centre has a shop, where you can buy some lovely Mouseman gifts.

Opening Times Showroom open all year 8am to 5pm (Monday to Thursday), 8am to 3.45pm (Friday), and 10am to 12 noon (Saturday). Visitor Centre: Easter to October 10am to 5pm daily (excluding Mondays in April, May and October).

Address Kilburn, York

Contact 01347 868218

 # Helmsley

The Bead Workshop

For a unique collection of hand-painted craft jewellery and hand-dyed silks visit The Bead Workshop at The Walled Garden.

Opening Times 10.30am to 4.30pm Tuesday to Sunday April 1 to October 31. Weekends only November and December.

Address The Walled Garden, Cleveland Way, Helmsley

Contact 01439 771123

Dolly Mix

My daughters have a wooden dolls house and so I was delighted to stumble across this little shop in Helmsley and chat with its owner Norma Johnson, who previously had a shop at Beverley.

Dolly Mix carries an array of stock, including some wonderful hand-crafted items that are made locally. There are even some tiny boxes of chocolates for dolls houses that have been made by Norma's daughter.

You can buy dolls houses and shops here and everything you need to transform them into the homes and shops of your dreams. Many of the items sold are too precious for little hands to get hold of, however, and are aimed more at collectors.

Opening Times Wednesday to Sunday inclusive. Closed Monday and Tuesday (except Bank Holiday weeks).

Address The Dolls House Shop, Cleveland Way, Helmsley

Contact 01439 771199

Hunters of Helmsley

The very best in Yorkshire food and drink is available at the high class delicatessen Hunters of Helmsley, a family business established in 1990.

Housed in a charming building that overlooks the Market Place, Hunters of Helmsley is a specialist shop and here you will find products belonging to Taylors of

Harrogate, Farrah's, Whitakers, Elizabeth Bothams, plus much, much more.

Opening Times Open seven days a week all year round, 8am to 5.30pm in winter, 8am to 7pm in summer. Closed Christmas Day and Boxing Day.

Address 13 Market Place, Helmsley

Contact 01439 771307

McLeods

Just outside the entrance to The Walled Garden you will find McLeods shop and its beautiful hand-smocked children's dresses that would aptly suit the young girl in the children's classic The Secret Garden with their traditional style and timeless appeal.

Fleeces and leggings are among other items available here.

Opening Times Open from Wednesday to Sunday inclusive (and often on other days as well).

Address The Walled Garden, Cleveland Way, Helmsley

Contact 01439 770881 • www.kids-clothing.co.uk

The Stick Man

The gift of a walking stick decorated with a labrador's head from his wife was to change the life of Keith Pickering, who was at the time working at a trout farm near Helmsley. For the stick inspired him to make one himself, bearing the head of a cock pheasant, it began a sequence of events that led to him to take up stick making full time.

His early work created so much interest that he gained the name 'the stick man' and in 1999 he hired a workshop at Helmsley Walled Garden and gave up his job at the trout farm. He now spends his time creating a fabulous range of sticks that feature all kinds of handles and heads, from deer antler to hardwood crooks and many animal, bird and fish head handles, including pheasant, grouse, duck, trout, fox and badger.

If you have a dog or horse Keith can carve a portrait of it from a photograph for a special walking stick, and he has carved sticks with family crests on them. Keith also runs training workshops, teaching people to make and carve their own sticks.

Royalty from all over Europe are among Keith's customers and during my visit he was working on a big order for a store in New York.

Opening Times You will find Keith at his workshop most days.

Address The Walled Garden, Cleveland Way, Helmsley

Contact 01439 771450

 *Hutton le Hole*

Moorwax candles

Hutton-le-Hole is a delightful little village and home to the workshop of candlemaker Chris Jones.

Chris has been making candles since 1972 and he uses only the finest quality waxes, including local beeswax, to produce a long lasting, clean burning candle. He aims to raise the level of candlemaking to an art form and his influences are modern ceramic glazes and natural colours and textures.

Each and every candle is handmade and decorated and the Moorwax range includes church candles, decorative candles, and special commissions.

Opening Times The Moorwax workshop is normally open 11am to 5pm Tuesday to Sunday from April to December. Please telephone at other times.

Address Wood View, Hutton-le-Hole

Contact 01751 417233

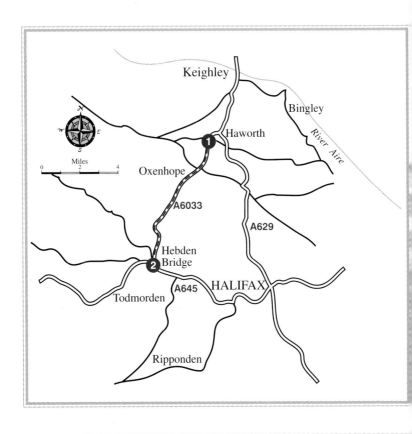

Brontë Country

Introduction

People from all over the world make pilgrimages to this area to see first-hand the life-long home of the famous literary family the Brontës and explore the Yorkshire moorland that inspired their writing.

Here you will also be reminded of the charming Hovis television commercial that was filmed in Haworth; the classic film *The Railway Children* was also made in the area.

Central to Haworth is its steep Main Street, where high street glitz has no place and stone sett paving is lined with a delightful mix of individual shops selling a fascinating range of wares.

Rose and Co Apothecary is enthralling with its old shop fittings displaying oils and balms, lotions and ointments, and a superb range of old-fashioned sweets. The Souk is a veritable Aladdin's Cave of textiles, jewellery and furniture. Sweetshops delight with their simple old-fashioned style, and cafés serving home-made fare line the street.

My favourite find here has to be Greenwoods Clog Shop, located just a short drive out of the centre of Haworth. You could be mistaken for thinking this little clog-making shop is a museum, but it is still making traditional clogs just as it has done since it was established in 1925.

Here in Haworth you can also take a trip on the Keighley and Worth Valley Railway, one of the country's best loved preserved steam railways.

Close by is The National Trust's East Riddlesden Hall, where you can take a look at 17th century life, and The Vintage Carriages Trust Museum of Rail Travel and Relics Shop at Ingrow Railway Centre near Keighley.

Take a trip to Hebden Bridge a few miles away and you will find an excellent choice of shops in what is an attractive and welcoming town.

 *Haworth*

Angels Lace Shop

A sea of white greets you at Angels Lace Shop in Haworth's Main Street. This shop specialises in the finest English guipure lace from Nottingham and stocks the best in linens, lace and napery from around the world.

There are exquisite christening gowns, bridal accessories, antique design nightdresses and beautiful heirlooms.

This shop was the original post office during the time of the Brontës and it was from here that their famous manuscripts were posted.

Opening Times 11am to 5pm seven days a week in the summer months, 12 noon to 5pm weekends in the winter months. Closed Christmas Day.

Address Main Street, Haworth

Contact 01535 642243

Mrs Beightons

Sweetshop owners love people like me who cannot resist the temptation of buying not just one bar of chocolate or packet of sweets, but instead have to pretend that those over and above the permissible amount for one individual is actually for their children! As a child I remember cycling to the sweet shop and buying a bag of sherbert pips or some other sugary delight assured to keep my dentist happy. It was memories of these childhood trips to the sweetshop that I was instantly reminded of when I walked through the door of Mrs Beightons in Haworth's Main Street for the first time – but not the last!

For Mrs Beightons is a traditional Yorkshire sweetshop in the very truest sense. The shop could be in a film set, its worn look is so reminiscent of a bygone age. There are no gaudy plastic shop stands, just wooden shop fittings and shelves filled with traditional jars of sweets, ranging from boiled sweets to liquorice, toffees, gums and pastilles, fudge, and kali and sherbert.

The deeds of the shop go back to 1682 and it is said this was one of the first buildings in Haworth. Its first known use as a shop was as a herbalist's and the then owner invented his own version of gentlemen's hair cream.

Mrs Beightons' best selling item is boiled sweets, which have been made in England since the late 19th century. Before its use in confectionery, the apothecaries or early chemists used sugar to sweeten and temper the taste of their medicines. Boiled sweets it appears evolved from sugar-coated pills and the like.

Lozenges, gums and pastilles came into existence around the turn of the century for treating sore throat and stomach complaints. Gradually these became popular without their medicinal benefits. And so the story of sweets goes on, making me want to nip out for some chocolate right now – apparently this came from Mexico in the form of cocoa as a drink by the Spanish in 1502.

You will enjoy Mrs Beightons – I did. If you get home and wish you had bought more the shop operates a much-used mail order service. That way no one will ever know just what a sweet tooth you have got!

Opening Times 10.30am to 5.30pm seven days a week.

Address 127 Main Street, Haworth

Contact 01535 642524 • www.mrsbeightonssweets.cwc.net

The Brontë Weaving Shed

Watch Brontë Tweed being created on a handloom in the traditional way as it was in the days of Queen Victoria when you visit The Brontë Weaving Shed at Haworth.

Here you will find an exhibition paying tribute to Timmy Feather, who was the last of Yorkshire's handloom weavers, and also see an impressive waterwheel that runs all day.

There are plenty of shopping opportunities. You can buy some of the famous Brontë Tweed, or choose from an array of knitwear and clothing.

Opening Times Seven days a week all year.

Address Townend Mill, Haworth

Contact 01535 646217

Greenwoods Clogs

Stepping into the tiny premises of Greenwoods Clogs you start to wonder when the little elves are going to appear. For this traditional clogmaker's which was established in 1925 is a magical place where all remains little changed in over three-quarters of a century.

The austerity of this small workshop that combines as a shop and the amazing spectacle of all the original pieces of equipment that are still in use today is a sheer delight to the eyes – and nose! There are rows of last after last in adult sizes down to the tiniest of sizes for young children, irons hanging, pots of nails, an ancient sewing machine which has apparently not improved in temperament with age, and many examples of the different styles of clogs you can have made.

My being able to enjoy this discovery is down to the latest owner of Greenwoods Clogs, Robin Longbottom, who bought the business from Ellis Greenwood, son of the founder, in November 1998. Ellis had decided to retire and close the shop, causing a great outcry among customers. Robin who lived close by and had visited the shop many times decided he wanted to keep the local tradition of clogmaking alive and approached Ellis. The sale was agreed, with Robin promising to keep the name and getting an 'apprenticeship' with Ellis in the craft of clogmaking thrown in.

Robin has a great passion for his new business and recounts its history with a quiet sense of pride. It was established by Harry Greenwood and was originally located a short distance from its existing site.

Harry set the business up after serving an apprenticeship with a clogmaker in Keighley and worked as a full-time clogmaker until the late seventies. Following his death his son Ellis thought he would honour all his father's orders and used the clogmaking skills he had acquired to make the clogs ordered. He ended up staying for over 20 years!

Robin said the decision to buy the business was initiated by his wife Josephine, who urged him to buy it. Many years ago they had spent a considerable amount of time trying to find some clogs for Josephine, but found that all the clog shops had closed down.

"When I was a kid there were dozens of them. Every village had a clog shop," said Robin.

He estimates there are around 18 clogmakers left in the country – in 1901 a total of 6,276 were recorded for England and Wales!

When Robin took over Greenwoods it coincided with his leaving his job and he spent eight months working full-time at the clog shop. He has since got a new job and now works at the shop on Saturdays and some evenings.

Clogs, with their wood soles, are said to be a very healthy footwear option and come in all sorts of styles. A 'duck toe' apparently is especially useful when walking up the likes of Haworth Main Street as the toe gives you that extra bit of turn.

"I just want to try and preserve it as a clog shop. People can go to a number of museums and see clogmaking equipment just like this on show, but they are just exhibits. This is a working shop which is still providing a service," said Robin.

It is obvious regular customers are delighted with the shop being saved. One delighted customer apparently threw open the door and exclaimed "Thank God". Others, who bought two and three pairs of clogs when Ellis said he was retiring, are just starting to return for new pairs.

Not only has Robin mastered the craft of clogmaking, Josephine has had a go, as too have their two sons, James and John.

If you need a pair of clogs this is the place to go, if not just pop in and enjoy the magic of Greenwoods Clogs. Prices of clogs range from £40 to £75.

Opening Times Greenwoods Clogs is open every Saturday from 9am until 12.30pm. Robin is more than happy to open up in the evenings for anyone interested in some clogs. Just telephone him on the number below.

Address 80 Haworth Road, Cross Roads, Haworth

Contact 01535 647100

Haworth Station Shop

A must for all train enthusiasts, this shop at Haworth Station sells a wide range of videos, books, magazines and souvenirs, as well as 'Thomas' and model railway items.

Haworth Station is one of the stops on the Keighley and Worth Valley Railway – Britain's last remaining complete branch line railway. Every weekend of the year, and daily in summer, you can take a memorable steam journey along the five-mile line and enjoy seeing the locations chosen by many film and television producers. The children's classic film *The Railway Children* was filmed here, along with *Yanks*, *Sherlock Holmes*, *Jude*, and many more.

Haworth Station is one of the Railway's six superbly restored gas-lit stations. The Railway also has it own fleet of steam locomotives and historic carriages.

Opening Times The shop at Haworth station is open 364 days a year.

Address Haworth Station, Haworth

Contact www.kwvr.co.uk

Rose and Co Apothecary

It is like stepping into a bygone era when you walk through the door of Rose and Co Apothecary in Haworth's Main Street and your eyes meet the wondrous old-fashioned interior while your nostrils savour the exotic oils, fragrances and soaps.

I still wonder at finding such a shop, which carries a fabulous and endless range of stock that I thought was no longer available – all displayed in a stunning range of rich old mahogany and glass display cases and other wonderful old shop fittings that include huge grocery bins. Glass globes provide warm light and old enamelled signs advertise the products of a bygone age.

Apparently the shop was the druggist's house and shop when the Brontë family lived at Haworth.

Today, the shop attracts many regular customers and wins the admiration and praise of its many visitors. It carries a huge amount of products, including oils, balms, salves, lotions, ointments and mixtures, and manufactures many of these on the premises. Rose and Co Apothecary has its own aromatherapist and produces a range of professionally blended essential oils, skin creams, therapeutic salts, handmade soaps, and ointments, balms and salves.

Alongside the traditional and old-fashioned you will find the best in contemporary bath and beauty products from England and around the world.

I love shops like this, where you can find rare and hard to find items delightfully packaged in tins, jars, bottles and boxes. Go to the rear of the shop and you will also find a lovely range of old sweets – many of which I again thought went out of production years ago.

Opening Times 10.30am to 5.30pm seven days a week, including Bank Holidays. Closed Christmas Day.

Address 84 Main Street, Haworth

Contact 01535 646830 • www.rose-apothecary.co.uk

The Souk

I walked into The Souk off Haworth's Main Street and was overwhelmed with the size of the interior and the fabulous range of old textiles, jewellery, linens and furniture on display.

This Aladdin's Cave houses an impressive collection of vintage clothing, from an 1830's day dress through to clothes from the 1940s.

There are also Victorian patchwork quilts and traditional rag rugs that are made by a local woman adding further to the sea of colour and textures that greets the visitor.

The building started off life as a Liberal Club and was more recently home to the Museum of Childhood. Dianne Bentley, who enjoys searching out unusual and sought-after items to sell there, now owns it.

Opening Times 11.30am until 6pm every day.

Address 117 Main Street, Haworth

Contact 01535 646538

Tabby's

If you are like me and adore farmhouse kitchens with all their rustic appeal you will enjoy a visit to Tabby's at Haworth. Here you can find terracotta cookware, Cornishware pottery, potbelly stoves and Belfast sink units all perfectly suited to the kitchens of farmhouses and country cottages – or to help you create such a look. There is also a lovely range of jams and chutneys.

Until recently Tabby's also displayed and sold a range of stunning oak furniture made by Haworth craftsman Christian Holmes. At the time of writing Christian was preparing to open his own shop next door to Tabby's. This 17th century style furniture that includes Yorkshire and Lancashire chairs is well worth seeing.

Opening Times 10am to 5pm Monday to Friday.

Address 89 Main Street, Haworth

Contact 01535 644407 • www.tabbys.co.uk

② *Hebden Bridge*

Mill Pottery

I remember visiting this workshop and being delighted to see a handwritten sign saying 'Please pick up the pots'. Makes a change from 'Don't touch' and 'All breakages must be paid for'.

You have to climb up a few stairs to Mill Pottery, where you can

see domestic stoneware and individual pieces by Jan Burgess. You can often see work in progress too.

Opening Times 9.30am to 5.30pm Monday to Saturday. Closed Sunday.

Address Bridge Mill Workshops, Hebden Bridge

Contact 01422 844559

The Pennine Wine and Cheese Company

All lovers of fine food and wine will like this Hebden Bridge shop – The Pennine Wine and Cheese Company.

Here you will find over 300 types of wine from around the globe, more than 120 different cheeses, and a fabulous selection of pastas, olives, antipasti, olive oils, vinegars, luxury chocolates, and much, much more. Continental breads are baked on the premises daily. If you are visiting the area and are feeling peckish, you will not find a better sandwich menu than here.

Opening Times 9am to 5.30pm Monday to Saturday. 11am to 5pm Sunday

Address 8 Bridge Gate, Hebden Bridge

Contact 01422 843121 • www.penninewine.co.uk

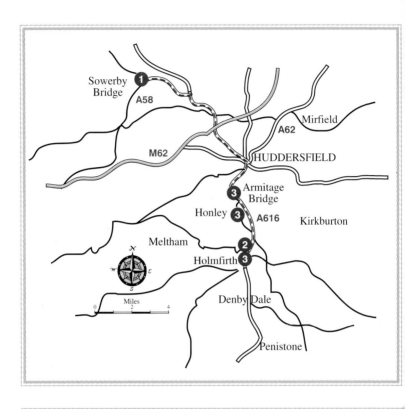

Summer Wine Country

Introduction

Compo, Clegg and Foggy will live on forever I suspect in the Pennine village of Holmfirth, where the BBC Television series *The Last of the Summer Wine* was filmed.

I remember at school being called 'Nora Batty' when my long socks wrinkled below my knees and here in Holmfirth is the 'Wrinkled Stocking Tearoom', named after the famous lady herself. There is also The Last of the Summer Wine Exhibition to visit, and Sid's Café of course.

It is true that the popular television series is responsible for many visitors coming to the area, but there is much more to the Holme Valley. Holmfirth, with its narrow alleys and ginnels, and weavers' cottages, is filled with interesting little shops and galleries. You can also enjoy a visit to the Holmfirth Postcard Collection.

The area boasts a thriving artistic community and there are studios and shops everywhere you go. The well-known landscape painter Ashley Jackson has a gallery here.

Holmfirth also has a regular craft market, where you can buy a wide range of crafts – many made locally.

A great discovery for me was Longley's shop, the first shop to be opened by J and E Dickinson, Longley Farm, and to see its new range of ice creams and fudge and toffee produced especially for the shop. All fellow Longley Farm devotees will no doubt share my enthusiasm at this particular shopping find.

This is a wonderful area to explore on foot, with the Peak Park starting only a few miles south of Holmfirth. Here you will find the dramatic landscape and peace and tranquillity that acts as inspiration to so many local artists.

 Sowerby Bridge

Spencers Trousers

If you have an active outdoor life and like to look your best playing golf, walking, or pursuing some other outdoor sporting or leisure activity, you would be well advised to visit the factory shop of Spencers Trousers.

This area of Yorkshire has long been associated with high quality cloth and trouser manufacturing and the tradition lives on today at Friendly Works.

Using locally sourced quality cotton and woollen cloth, Spencers Trousers create a range of trouser styles in various materials, including natural fibres and a variety of traditional tweeds and tartans. They carry an amazing 400 tartan designs alone.

Whether you want trousers, plus twos, plus fours, breeches or tailored shorts, in either men's or women's sizes, you can get them here. All garments are individually hand cut.

Opening Times 9am to 5pm Monday to Saturday.

Address Friendly Works, Burnley Road, Sowerby Bridge

Contact 01422 833020 • www.spencers-trousers.com

 Holmfirth

Beatties Delicatessen

The last time I was in Holmfirth I sought refuge during a shower at Beatties Delicatessen, which is opposite the famous Sid's Café. Here at Beatties I totally forgot any thoughts of the weather when I received my ordered smoked ham, Brie and redcurrant jelly hot baguette in the adjoining café area. It was delicious.

I also took the opportunity to look round the delicatessen, which

offers a superb range of scrumptious fare, including handmade preserves, chutneys and mustard.

Opening Times 9.30am to 5pm Monday to Saturday, 10am to 5pm Sunday.

Address 6 Town Gate, Holmfirth

Contact 01484 689000

Holmfirth Craft Market

Holmfirth Market, Holmfirth

I love markets – they offer so much variety and many surprises. Here in Holmfirth every Saturday and Bank Holiday Monday from March through to Christmas you will find over 30 stalls of handcrafted goods at the Holmfirth Craft Market.

Longley Farm

For years I have been a devoted fan of Longley Farm yoghurts, with a particular liking for the hazelnut variety. In fact, these yoghurts are my family's staple dessert and in my opinion are simply the best.

With the above in mind imagine my delight at finding a newly-opened Longley Farm shop in Holmfirth – Longley's – selling items produced at the well known local dairy, including a new range of ice creams and fudge and toffee produced especially for the shop. Heaven!

J and E Dickinson, Longley Farm, Holmfirth, is an independent dairy built on a history of traditional values and a commitment to quality. The business was started by Joseph Dickinson and Edgar Dickinson in 1948, although records connect the Dickinson family to Longley Farm as far back as the early 17th century.

Initially a farm, it became a dairy in 1954, the year that rationing ended. Joseph's son Jim Dickinson now runs the business, which is famed for its superb range of natural quality products. These range from cream and fromage frais to butter and yoghurt.

Longley Farm has its own large Jersey herd and employs 150 people at its Holmfirth factory.

Although many Longley Farm products are available far and wide, many of the items sold at the new Longley's shop can only be bought there. So what are you waiting for.

Opening Times 9.30am to 5.30pm Tuesday to Friday, 9.30am to 6pm Saturday, 11am to 6pm Sunday. Closed Monday.

Address Huddersfield Road, Holmfirth

Contact 01484 681252 • www.longleyfarm.com

Rowan Up Country

Established in Holmfirth for 16 years, this colourful shop offers far more than the strong visual appeal of its busy interior. Here you can find a superb range of quality knitting products, including Rowan and Jaegar knitting yarns, magazines and designs.

There is also a range of lovely ready-to-wear knitwear and some very stylish womenswear in linen and cotton. Other items available here include hats and scarves, handmade jewellery, bags, cushions and cards.

Opening Times 9.30am to 5pm Monday to Saturday. Open the first Sunday of each month 1am to 4pm.

Address 6 Market Walk, Holmfirth

Contact 01484 687803 • www.upcountry.co.uk

Smilecraft

You can let your imagination run wild in Smilecraft, a shop that specialises in dolls houses and miniatures. You can conjure up any world you wish using the endless range of items stocked in this fascinating shop that can be found down an old cobbled walkway.

Run by Sue and Geoff Pike it offers everything you could ever need to create a magical world in miniature. Adults and children alike will love visiting here.

Opening Times 10am to 4pm Tuesday to Saturday. Closed Sunday and Monday.

Address 7 Norridge Bottom, Holmfirth

Contact 01484 689086

③ *Summer Wine Gallery Trail*

The Summer Wine area is rich with art galleries, each one offering a unique world of individual art and crafts in welcoming surroundings.

Ashley Jackson Galleries

Thanks to well-known Yorkshire artist Ashley Jackson an ever-increasing number of people are able to share in the wonders of paint on canvas and an appreciation of the beauties of the landscape around them.

For Ashley is a man of the people and at every opportunity takes his passion for painting into the public domain and allows others to both enjoy and be inspired by it.

His Yorkshire Television series A Brush with Ashley has proved a great success and his reputation as an artist with great talent both for painting and promoting the art continues to grow apace. From May to September 2000 he celebrated his 60th birthday with an exhibition called 'Dawn's a New Day' at the Royal Armouries Museum, Leeds – admission was free.

Holmfirth is fortunate to be home to the

Ashley Jackson Galleries. This is the only UK outlet where you can view his original collection.

Ashley Jackson needs little introduction. Elected a Fellow of the Royal Society of Arts in 1967, he has exhibited his works around the globe, appeared on many television shows, and brought us some wonderful books on the subject he is so passionate about. His latest book is *Ashley Jackson's Yorkshire Moors – A Love Affair*, published by Dalesman.

He has won the affection of a large audience over the years, but always appears unaffected by it and very content with life. In 1996 he was honoured with the 'Yorkshire Arts and Entertainment Personality of the Year' award, and in 1987 His Royal Highness the Prince of Wales opened his one man exhibition called 'Ashley Jackson's Vision of Turner in Yorkshire'.

Opening Times 9.30am to 5pm Monday to Saturday. Closed Sundays.

Address 13/15 Huddersfield Road, Holmfirth

Contact 01484 686460 • www.ashley-jackson.co.uk

Lupton Square Gallery

A spiral staircase and light airy rooms spread over three floors are features of the appealing Lupton Square Gallery at Honley – located in a beautifully renovated 18th century house.

Here you will find a wide range of quality works of art and craft, including paintings, ceramics, sculpture and original prints. Displays are changing constantly, so there is always something new to see.

There is a lovely feel to this gallery and it offers a relaxed and welcoming environment in which to enjoy the work on show.

Opening Times 10am to 5pm every Friday, Saturday, Sunday and Bank Holidays.

Address 1 and 2 Lupton Square, Honley

Contact 01484 666144

North Light Gallery

It is not only the north light that is shining on this superb new gallery, where you can see the best of British contemporary art displayed in the spacious surroundings of part of the redeveloped historic Armitage Bridge Mills.

Opened in 2000, it has already been described as "the most exciting gallery in the north" and is able to show off large-scale paintings and sculpture in a way that only such an expansive gallery can.

The former textile mill complex where the gallery is located is now the Yorkshire Technology and Office Park – home to an array of creative industries – and is still owned by the Brooke family who founded their firm in 1541.

A gallery café allows you to sit and relax over a cup of coffee and perhaps some sandwiches and cakes supplied by the WI, and enjoy seeing the latest exhibition of paintings or sculptures. There is also a changing programme of music, dance and practical workshops, which you may like to join in.

The North Light Gallery is a wonderful and welcome addition to the area and will no doubt become a favourite with many people – and with artists themselves.

Opening Times 11am to 5pm Wednesday to Friday, 11am to 4pm Saturday.

Address Yorkshire Technology Park, Armitage Bridge, Huddersfield

Contact 01484 340003

Sanderson George and Peach

Regular customers at the Sanderson George and Peach contemporary art gallery in Holmfirth include cast members from various well-known television programmes filmed locally, and it is easy to see what appeals to them about this gallery and its contents.

A double fronted Victorian shop, the building itself has many wonderful original features that have been carefully yet simply restored to provide a sympathetic backdrop to the many and varied works on display.

Based in Holmfirth, an area rich with professional artists and crafts people, the gallery represents and supports many local artists, including a number who now work in its many studio spaces. Regular exhibitors include Brendan Hesmondhalgh, Jane Strawbridge, Mick Kirby Geddes and Jo Aylward. Artists range from the newly-established to the well-known and long-established designers and craft workers.

The gallery was originally established in April 1996 by Andrew Sanderson a photographer, Debbie George a painter, and Amanda Peach a gallery co-ordinator. Catherine Hill joined in September 1998 from a background in arts and primary education and Debbie and Catherine now form the sole partnership and have expanded the business to double its original size.

Well worth the short walk from the centre of Holmfirth.

Opening Times 10am to 5pm Tuesday to Saturday.

Address 39 Station Road, Holmfirth

Contact 01484 684485

Other galleries in this area that you may like to visit include:

The Rosalind Annis Gallery

Hollogate, Holmfirth
Contact: 01484 688774
Opening Times: 10.30am to 5pm Tuesday and Saturday.

Booth House Gallery

3 Booth House, Holmfirth
Contact: 01484 685270
Opening Times: 1pm to 5pm Saturday and Sunday. Check
midweek times by phone.

Trevor Stubley Gallery

Greenfield Road, Holmfirth
Contact: 01484 682026
It is advisable to telephone first before visiting.

Susan Brown

The Crown Park Lane, Birds Edge
Contact: 01484 603769
Opening Times: 10am to 6pm Thursday to Friday, and 10am to
4pm Saturday.

White Rose Gallery

Daisy Lane, Holmfirth
Contact: 01484 688408
Opening Times: 9am to 5pm Monday and Wednesday to Saturday,
10am to 5pm Sunday.